THE AMERICAN PUBLIC LIBRARY AND THE PROBLEM OF PURPOSE

Recent Titles in
Contributions in Librarianship and Information Science
Series Editor: Paul Wasserman

THE AMERICAN PUBLIC LIBRARY AND THE PROBLEM OF PURPOSE

Patrick Williams

Contributions in Librarianship and Information Science, Number 62

GREENWOOD PRESS
New York • Westport, Connecticut • London

Library of Congress Cataloging-in-Publication Data

Williams, Patrick, 1930-
    The American public library and the problem of purpose / Patrick
Williams.
        p.   cm.—(Contributions in librarianship and information
science, ISSN 0084–9243 ; no. 62)
    Bibliography: p.
    Includes index.
    ISBN 0-313-25590-3 (lib. bdg. : alk. paper)
        1. Public libraries—United States—History.   2. Public libraries—
United States—Aims and objectives.   3. Libraries and society—
United States.   4. Library administration—United States—History.
I. Title.   II. Series.
Z731.W735 1988
027.473—dc 19   88-16382

British Library Cataloguing in Publication Data is available.

Library of Congress Catalog Card Number: 88-16382
ISBN: 0-313-25590-3
ISSN: 0084-9243

First published in 1988

Greenwood Press, Inc.
88 Post Road West, Westport, Connecticut 06881

Printed in the United States of America

The paper used in this book complies with the
Permanent Paper Standard issued by the National
Information Standards Organization (Z39.48-1984).

10   9   8   7   6   5   4   3   2   1

To Nancy

Contents

Preface

This book is a historical essay dealing with the efforts of public librarians and others seriously concerned with the institution to find the right place for the public library in American life. Finding that place is the problem of purpose to which the title refers.

Finding the right place means, first of all, developing an idea of purpose that identifies a distinctive and valuable contribution that the library can reasonably be expected to make with the resources that society can reasonably be expected to provide. In addition, finding the right place means choosing and developing the instruments, such as collections and services, through which the contribution is made.

For more than 130 years, the public library community has struggled with the problem of finding the right place for the library, the problem of purpose. This book is a chronicle of that struggle. It begins with a discussion of the Boston Public Library and ends with a discussion of the very recent past. The intent is to provide a measure of historical understanding that will help those in the public library community who will struggle with the problem in the future.

I have had a lot of help writing this book. My wife Nancy and my sons, Jay and Patrick, read the typescript and made many recommendations that were helpful to say the least. Mary Sue Brown, the director of the Woodridge, Illinois, Public Library, also read the typescript and offered valuable criticism and advice. I must also thank the Rosary College community for encouragement and support and the librarians in particular for the hard labor they cheerfully performed.

THE AMERICAN
PUBLIC LIBRARY AND
THE PROBLEM OF
PURPOSE

1

The Boston Prototype

1841–1878

The modern history of the American public library began in Boston. On March 20, 1854, the doors of a rented schoolhouse, temporary quarters of a brand new library, opened to the citizens of Boston so that they might begin to enjoy the benefits the founders sought to provide. The citizens of Boston had been waiting a long time.

Almost thirty years earlier, in 1826, an idea for a public library was set forth by George Ticknor, a Harvard professor and prominent citizen. Ticknor's plan was to unite several of Boston's privately owned libraries into a single institution open to the public. But the project never got beyond the planning stage and was abandoned.

Some fifteen years later, a very different kind of man with a similar idea arrived in Boston. Alexandre Vattemare, a native of France, was neither an intellectual nor an aristocrat. He had spent most of his adult life as a performer in the popular theaters of Paris and other European capitals earning great acclaim as a ventriloquist. In recent years, Vattemare had given up the stage and was devoting what remained of his life to a great intellectual and cultural project.

Vattemare proposed that the great cities of the world exchange books and works of art and create libraries and museums in order to to present them to the public. He was a persuasive and inspiring speaker; he convinced people in many cities that his project was practical and would have the desired result. The response he evoked was seen in a resolution passed by one of his audiences: "We regard the system of national interchange suggested by Mr. Vattemare, as one which will tend to remove national and sectional prejudices, will promote the great cause of peace, and the first principle of religion, by uniting all nations in intellectual brotherhood; and one which . . . will bring about a kind of mental commerce which cannot fail to promote universal civilization."[1]

In September 1839, Vattemare sailed to North America to promote his project in Canada and the United States. He went to Montreal, Washington (where he addressed Congress), New York, and other cities. He arrived in Boston in April 1841. On May 5, he addressed an assembly of city leaders including the mayor.

Vattemare proposed a merger of the city's libraries into a single institution that would participate in international exchange. The union would have created an impressive institution. Boston had many fine libraries. The Boston Athenaeum, a library owned by five hundred stockholders, was one of the largest and best in the country; and more than a dozen other libraries owned fine collections of historical, scientific, and technical materials. Vattemare's audience was moved as usual. A committee of those present was formed to consider what might be done.

The committee decided to write to libraries, institutes and learned societies, fifteen in all, to test their willingness to cooperate in the following plan. A public building would be built to house books, works of art, specimens of natural history, and lecture and meeting rooms. The fifteen institutions would hand over their books and other collections and titles of ownership thereto. Continuing financial support for the new institution would be provided by donations, rents, and a tax based on "the same principle which now induces the citizens to tax themselves for the support of public schools."[2]

The response was that normally received by people who ask others to turn over their property. The Athenaeum said there were insuperable objections that were unnecessary to state in detail; three other bodies courteously declined to participate; ten more did not even respond. The one body that strongly favored the idea, the Mechanic Apprentices Library Association, had little to contribute.

Enthusiasm for the project evaporated. Vattemare returned to Europe. In 1843, he sent Boston a gift of fifty books from the city of Paris; he had not given up.

In 1847, Vattemare returned to Boston. He no longer hoped for a merger of Boston libraries. On this trip he tried to persuade Boston officials to establish a city library. The mayor, Josiah Quincy, wholeheartedly supported this idea. That same year, another gift of books arrived from Paris. The Boston city council appointed a committee consisting of Mayor Quincy and several aldermen to consider what to do with the gifts. This committee issued a report recommending that the city council consider establishing a public library. The council then appointed a special committee on the public library; and on December 6, 1847, that committee reported that a public library would indeed be useful but did not propose that public money be spent on it.

Mayor Quincy was not satisfied, and in January 1848 he persuaded a new city council to apply to the state legislature for authorization to establish and maintain a public library. On March 18, the legislature authorized Boston

to establish a library and to apropriate up to $5,000 a year for library pur-
poses.

   With such a small sum to spend, Mayor Quincy was receptive to a proposal
received from the trustees of the Athenaeum in the summer of 1848. The
trustees proposed to open that library to the public. The city was to give
the Athenaeum a single payment of $50,000, to be raised by public sub-
scription, plus a annual subsidy of $5,000. This plan, however, was subject
to the approval of the five hundred stockholders who actually owned the
Athenaeum; they rejected the idea. Just how the Boston Public Library would
come into existence was still unclear.

   In April 1849, Vattemare was again in Boston. He brought another gift
of books from Paris. Some of the titles indicated ·that the Parisians found
Vattemare's exchange program a useful opportunity for weeding their collections. Included were *Accounts of the Public Pawn-Brokers, from 1841 to 1844*
(2 volumes), *Reports on the Progress and Effects of the Cholera Morbus in the City
of Paris and the Department of the Seine in 1832, Reports . . . by the Special Committee
Appointed for the Organization of Slaughter-Houses, and the Regulation of Butcheries*
(1843), *Regulations Concerning the Sale of Spiritous Drinks* (1837), *Statistical Map
of the Sewers of the City of Paris* (1839).[3]

   Boston received these with gratitude and prepared a gift for Paris. Boston's
gift included works by Emerson, Longfellow and Whittier; and mindful
perhaps of what Paris had sent, the Bostonians included a Burmese edition
of a trigonometry text, a Siamese *New Testament*, and some publications of
the Massachusetts Sabbath School Society including *Louisa Ralston, or What
Can I Do for the Heathen?*[4]

   This exchange of gifts marked the end of Vattemare's involvement in the
creation of the Boston Public Library, an involvement both serious and comic.
The inspiration he gave was serious, especially the drive imparted to Josiah
Quincy. Not everyone was impressed by Vattemare, however; many thought
him a charlatan. He clearly had some strange ideas: he once recommended
that San Francisco send Paris an alligator in exchange for a cast of the Venus
de Milo. On the whole, however, Vattemare seems to deserve the credit he
has traditionally received as an important contributor to the founding of the
Boston Public Library.

   Despite the failure of the Athenaeum project of 1848, leading citizens of
Boston continued to believe that a public library would eventually exist.
Through 1849, individuals donated books and documents that joined the
collection raised by Vattemare's efforts, a collection gathering dust in city
hall. In 1850, Mayor Bigelow, Quincy's successor, contributed the first gift
of cash, one thousand dollars. That same year, Edward Everett, formerly
president of Harvard, governor of Massachusetts, and Minister to the Court
of St. James, offered a thousand volumes of valuable documents. The city
council undertook to receive them when it could provide a suitable place.
News of Everett's gift revived the interest of George Ticknor in creating a

public library in Boston. Finally, a combination of the enabling legislation of 1848, the accumulating gifts, and the pressure of civic leaders led to concrete steps.

In February 1852, Mayor Bigelow's successor, Benjamin Seaver, asked the city council to appoint a librarian and board of trustees. In May, a former clergyman, Edward Capen, was appointed librarian. There was a problem, however, concerning the board. The services of both Everett and Ticknor were wanted; but Ticknor was unwilling to serve unless assured that the library would freely circulate books. He was aware of the doubts that Everett had concerning that practice. Everett yielded, and Ticknor took his place on the thirteen-member board. At the first board meeting on May 31, 1852, a committee consisting of Everett, Ticknor, and three others was appointed to write a report on "the objects to be attained by the establishment of a public library and the best mode of effecting them."[5]

In July 1852, the committee presented its report, most of which was written by Ticknor. The report was a lengthy theoretical justification for the creation of a new public institution. The library was to serve the city of Boston as an educational institution, an adjunct to the public schools. The report stated:

The system of public education in Boston may probably sustain a comparison with any in the world . . . The schools . . . give a first rate school education, at the public expense, to the entire rising generation. But when this object is attained . . . our system of public instruction stops . . . the public makes no provision whatever, by which the hundreds of young persons annually educated, as far as the elements of learning are concerned, at the public expense, can carry on their education and bring it to practical results by private study. . . . Why should not this prosperous and liberal city extend some reasonable amount of aid to the foundation and support of a noble public library, to which the young people of both sexes, when they leave the schools, can resort for those works which pertain to general culture, or which are needful for research into any branch of useful knowledge? . . . We consider that a large public library is of the utmost importance as the means of completing our system of public education . . . The trustees would endeavor to make the public library of the city, as far as possible, the crowning glory of our system of city schools . . . fitted to continue and increase the best effects of that system, by opening to all the means of self culture through books.[6]

The report emphasized the importance of a complete system of public education:

There can be no doubt that . . . reading ought to be furnished to all, as a matter of public policy and duty, on the same principle that we furnish free education. . . . It has been rightly judged that, under political, social and religious institutions like ours, it is of paramount importance that the means of general information should be so diffused that the largest possible number of persons should be induced to read and understand questions going down to the very foundations of social order, which are constantly presenting themselves, and which we, as a people, are constantly required to decide, and do decide, either ignorantly or wisely. That this can be done, that is, that such libraries can be collected, and that they will be used to a much wider extent than libraries have ever been used before, and with much more important results, there can be no doubt; and if it can be done anywhere, it can be done here in Boston.[7]

The trustees' report described the kinds of books the library would offer. There were three major categories: reference books, "books that few persons will wish to read," and popular books. The trustees were aware that many popular books were of dubious educational value; but they would be useful in cultivating a taste for reading. Once cultivated, the taste for reading would transform those who had acquired it. Readers of popular books would become readers of serious books.

When . . . a taste for books has once been formed by these lighter publications, then the older and more settled works in biography, in history, and in the graver departments of knowledge will be demanded. That such a taste can be excited by such means is proved from the course taken in obedience to the dictates of their own interests by the publishers of the popular literature of the time during the last twenty or thirty years. The Harpers and others began chiefly with new novels and other books of little value. What they printed, however, was eagerly bought and read, because it was cheap and agreeable, if nothing else. A habit of reading was thus formed. Better books were soon demanded, and gradually the general taste has risen in its requisitions, until now the country abounds with respectable works of all sorts . . . which are read by great numbers of our people everywhere. . . . This taste, therefore, once excited will, we are persuaded, go on of itself from year to year, demanding better and better books, and can, as we believe . . . be carried much higher than has been commonly deemed possible.[8]

The report closed with a proposal that the ground floor of a school on Mason Street be made available. The room would hold four or five thousand volumes. Its use would enable the library to open without excessive delay.

The trustees' report had one unexpected result. By good luck, a copy of the report was included with other papers sent to a London bank with which Boston was trying to negotiate a loan. A senior officer of the bank was a wealthy expatriate Bostonian, Joshua Bates. As a boy who craved books but was too poor to buy any, Bates had been allowed by friendly owners of a Boston bookstore to spend his evenings reading from their stock. The trustees' report made him think what a public library would have meant to him. Wishing to help establish such a library without delay, Bates wrote to the mayor on October 1, 1852, offering to buy the necessary bookstock and additions to it for as long as he lived. He estimated that $50,000 would suffice. The offer was gratefully accepted. The city council, however, asked permission to invest the money and use the income to create a book fund. Permission was granted. Final arrangements for opening the library were completed, and on March 20, 1854, the Boston Public Library opened its doors on Mason Street.

The Mason Street quarters were too small from the outset. Before the end of 1854, a decision was made to build a library that would accommodate about 240,000 volumes, a collection larger than any then existing in the country. The site was to be on Boylston Street. A little more than three years later, on New Year's Day, 1858, the new building was dedicated.

The new building was not huge, but it was large and grand enough to be called monumental. The interior had two large halls, the Lower Hall and directly above it the Upper Hall. Each was intended for a separate function. The Upper Hall was intended for serious readers. It had an open area thirty-eight by ninety-two feet plus space for shelving 200,000 volumes. The ceiling was fifty-eight feet above the floor. The Lower Hall was designed for the popular collection. There was space for shelving 40,000 volumes, for seating three hundred readers, and for a delivery room. A printed catalog of the Lower Hall collection, then 15,000 volumes, was finished, and books began to circulate from the Lower Hall on December 20, 1858. The Upper Hall was not ready for general public use until 1861.

The collection of 15,000 volumes assembled in the popular library of the Lower Hall in late 1858 was described by Charles Jewett, the superintendent of the library who had come to Boston from the Smithsonian Institution. The popular library, Jewett said, included works on science and technology as well as the writings of Hamilton, Jefferson, and the theologian Jonathan Edwards. Most of the books, Jewett acknowledged, were "of a more popular character": biography, fiction, history, and accounts of travels. But on the whole, Jewett said, the collection was "eminently suited to promote the ultimate design of the institution, the intellectual and moral advancement of the whole people."[9]

The trustees of the library apparently thought that intellectual advancement was a process that worked quickly. In 1859, the purchase of popular novels was curtailed. The trustees seemed to think that the public was demanding better things. "The next year there was a marked falling off in circulation."[10]

In 1866, a new charging system was installed and, for the first time, accurate circulation counts were available. The 1866 circulation from the popular library in the Lower Hall totaled 183,714. Of that number, at least 70 percent was fiction.

The chairman of the committee that did an annual analysis of library operations commented on the high percentage. This chairman happened to be Justin Winsor, a trustee who would eventually succeed Jewett as superintendent. The high percentage of fiction, Winsor said, might "alarm" some people. But if fiction was not supplied to the masses, it was likely that they would read nothing at all. Once the masses were accustomed to reading, there was a "fair chance" they would seek better books.[11]

In 1871, having been superintendent for about three years, Winsor commented again on the heavy circulation of popular fiction, calling it "inevitable." Libraries will always circulate large quantities of inferior fiction because that is what the masses "crave." It "sometimes happens" that readers advance to higher levels. But new readers, beginning "at the levels from which the old readers advanced" will "keep up the relative debasement."[12]

Winsor was not very optimistic. He spoke of a "fair chance" that novel readers might seek better books and acknowledged that readers "sometimes" advance to higher levels. But he was clearly skeptical about the taste-elevation theory that represented the official position of the Boston Public Library.

That position was restated in 1878 in the report of the committee that audited library operations. The committee, responding to the accusation that the library bought too many works of inferior fiction, said: "Banish them from the library, as some advise, and you banish their readers also. Keep them in the library and you keep their readers also; who with constantly improving taste, will finally select books of unquestionable excellence and profit."[13] The committee affirmed the position of the original board of trustees. The library is an educational institution, an adjunct to the public schools; it opens to all the citizens of Boston "the means of self culture through books."[14] The majority of the people crave fiction; but this is a temporary condition. Public taste will improve. Eventually, the public will demand "books of unquestionable excellence and profit."[15]

But what if the public did no such thing? What if taste did not improve and the public continued to want fiction of a low order? Then, it would appear, there was a defect in the original theory. That theory allowed the distribution of huge quantities of popular books because those books played a role in the library's education program. If it turned out that popular books played no such role, then some other justification for supplying them ought to be found. If such a justification could not be found, there would be a problem. It would be difficult to maintain that the library is an educational institution if it had to be acknowledged that the vast majority of the books supplied had no educational value.

But in Boston in the mid–1870s, there was, as yet, no serious problem. There was no serious doubt that the taste of the people would improve. It was only a question of time.

The Boston Public Library of the 1870s seemed to more than fulfill its founders' dreams. By 1877, the last year of the Winsor superintendency, the collection had grown to more than 300,000 volumes; total circulation exceeded one million; the library had six branches. It was the largest library in the country, the most used, and probably the best. The next decade would see an even grander plan realized. In 1888, the cornerstone was laid for the great library that now stands in Copley Square.

Meanwhile, the institution that Boston had created began appearing in other cities around the country. By 1875, 188 public libraries had been established, and many more were in the planning stages. The new libraries were faithful to the Boston prototype. They were educational institutions, their purpose symbolized in temple-of-learning architecture. If any problem arose concerning their educational value or effectiveness, all of them would face the problem together.

NOTES

1. Walter Muir Whitehill, *Boston Public Library: A Centennial History* (Cambridge: Harvard University Press, 1956), 6.

2. Ibid., 7.

3. Ibid., 16.

4. Ibid., 16–17.

5. Boston, *Report of the Trustees of the Public Library of the City of Boston* (Boston: 1852), 3. The complete text of the report is given in an appendix to Jesse H. Shera, *Foundations of the Public Library: The Origins of the Public Library Movement in New England* (Chicago: University of Chicago Press, 1949), 268–90.

6. Boston, *Report of the Trustees of the Public Library of the City of Boston*, 6–9, 21.

7. Ibid., 15.

8. Ibid., 17–18.

9. Whitehill, *Boston Public Library*, 58.

10. Ibid., 72.

11. Ibid., 73–74.

12. Ibid., 82–83.

13. Ibid., 120.

14. Boston, *Report of the Trustees of the Public Library of the City of Boston*, 21.

15. Whitehill, *Boston Public Library*, 120.

2

The Fiction Problem

1876–1896

In the last quarter of the nineteenth century, municipal public libraries became a standard American institution. As libraries increased in number, the new professional community of public librarians grew larger. The new community founded an association and a journal, created new forms of library service, and produced ingenious and lasting achievements in library technology. The years from 1876 to 1900 were years of growth and progress.

During those same years, the professional community came to realize that the public's preference for books of little or no educational value was an enduring one. Librarians ceased to believe in the taste-elevation theory, which argued that books of little or no educational value should be supplied to library users because such books are necessary at the earliest stage of self-education. They are attractive to readers who otherwise would read nothing. If such books are supplied, their readers will gradually lose their taste for them and demand books of educational value.

During the last quarter of the nineteenth century, as disbelief in the taste-elevation theory spread, librarians engaged in a long controversy over what to do about popular fiction. That controversy is the principal subject of this chapter.

The period opened with a series of promising events. During the first week in October 1876, ninety men and thirteen women met at a convention of librarians in Philadelphia. The leaders of the group were Justin Winsor of the Boston Public Library, William Frederick Poole, librarian of the Chicago Public Library, Charles A. Cutter of the Boston Athenaeum, and Melvil Dewey, librarian at Amherst College. Among the librarians at the convention, there were thirteen from academic libraries, forty-three from private and special libraries, and twenty-four from public libraries. Although public librarians were a minority, "it was they who controlled the convention."[1] The group assembled in Philadelphia founded the American Library Association (ALA). The public library community gained a measure of unity and organization.

In the same year, the *Library Journal* began publication. It was a product of the efforts of Melvil Dewey and Frederick Leypoldt of *Publishers' Weekly*. The journal quickly became the newsletter and forum of the public library community, the principal link between its far-flung members.

Another important event occurred in 1876: the publication of a huge report (1187 pages) entitled *Public Libraries in the United States of America: Their History, Condition and Management*. It was issued by the U.S. Bureau of Education, then a unit of the Department of the Interior. The report owed its creation to the belief of John Eaton, then the bureau's chief, that libraries were of great educational importance. In the report, which was essentially an essay collection with a statistical appendix, Eaton assembled the ideas of top library experts of the time: Winsor, Dewey, Poole, Cutter, and about twenty others. The report was the original American encyclopedia of library science.

There was no indication in the report that a controversy was soon to engage the members of the public library community. There was agreement that the library is an educational institution and that libraries lend popular fiction for educational purposes.

On the subject of purpose, William F. Poole, in an essay entitled "The Organization and Management of Public Libraries," wrote:

The public library . . . is established by state laws, is supported by local taxation and voluntary gifts, is managed as a public trust, and every citizen . . . has an equal share in its privileges of reference and circulation. It is not a library simply for scholars and professional men . . . but for the whole community, the mechanic, the laboring man, the sewing-girl, the youth, and all who desire to read. . . . It is the adjunct and supplement of the common school system. Both are established and maintained on the same principles: that general education is essential to the highest welfare of any people.[2]

William I. Fletcher, a public librarian from Hartford, Connecticut, contributed an essay entitled "Public Libraries in Manufacturing Communities." Public libraries, according to Fletcher, are "those libraries which are maintained as a part of the regular educational system, free to all, and supported by taxation."[3] J. P. Quincy, son of the Boston mayor inspired by Vattemare, in his contribution entitled "Free Libraries," took the same position.[4] There was no dissenting opinion in the report.

In their treatment of the role of fiction in the library's educational program, the authors affirmed the taste-elevation theory. William F. Poole, in the essay quoted earlier, wrote:

The masses of the public have very little of literary culture, and it is the purpose of a public library to develop it by creating in them a habit of reading. As a rule, people read books of a higher intellectual and moral standard than their own, and hence are benefited by reading. As their tastes improve they read better books. Books which are not adapted to their intellectual capacity they will not read. To meet, therefore, the varied wants of readers there must be on the shelves of the library books which persons of culture never read. ... Judged from a critical standpoint, such books are feeble, rudimentary, and perhaps sensational; but they are higher in the scale of literary merit than the tastes of the people who seek them; and like primers and first-readers in the public schools, they fortunately lead to something better.[5]

William Fletcher's contribution indicated that he had heard other opinions; but he rejected them:

No question connected with public libraries has been so much discussed, or is of such generally recognized importance, as that of the kinds of reading to be furnished. On the one hand, all kinds of arguments ... have been urged against the admission of any but the very highest order of fictitious works; while, on the other hand, the sweeping assertion is made by some that the public library cannot refuse to supply whatever the public sentiment calls for. The mean between these two extremes is doubtless the true view of the case. The managers of the public library are no less bound to control and shape the institution in their charge ... than are the managers of the school system. To say that calls for books should be accepted as the indications of what should be furnished, is to make their office a merely mechanical and per- functory one. ... Adherence to such a principle as this would make the library a mere slop shop of sensational fiction. But ... the entire exclusion of fiction of a sensational cast ... will unavoidably result in alienating from the library the very class most needing its beneficial influence. ... Let the library, then, contain just enough of the mere confectionery of literature to secure the interest in it of readers of the lowest— not depraved—tastes; but let this be so dealt out as may best make it serve its main purpose of a stepping stone to something better.[6]

F. B. Perkins, a colleague of Winsor's at the Boston Public Library, also treated the matter of fiction. In an essay entitled "How To Make Town Libraries Successful," he wrote:

The first mistake likely to be made in establishing a public library is choosing books of too thoughtful or solid a character. ... The only practical method is to begin by supplying books that people already want to read, and afterwards to do whatever shall be found possible to elevate their reading tastes and habits. ... "Silly reading," "trash," ... must to a considerable extent be supplied by the public library. And those who intend ... to exclude such "trash" might as well stop before they begin. But what is trash to some, is, if not nutriment, at least stimulus to others. Readers improve; if it were not so, reading would not be a particularly useful practice. The habit of reading is the first and indispensable step. That habit once established, it is a recognized fact that readers go from poorer to better sorts of reading. ... Those who begin with dime novels and story weeklies may be expected to grow into a liking for a better sort of stories; then for the truer narratives of travels and adventure, of biography and history, then of essays and popular science, and so on upward.

Concerning this upward progress, Perkins said, "the experience of librarians is substantially unanimous."[7]

Justin Winsor's contribution to the report was a two-page essay entitled "Reading in Popular Libraries." He called upon librarians to supply popular novels. But he viewed the taste-elevation process as one that depended upon the guidance of librarians. In this essay, Winsor seemed more optimistic than usual. Librarians, Winsor said, should:

> strive to elevate the taste of their readers, and this they can do, not by refusing to put within their reach the books which the masses of readers want, but by inducing a habit of frequenting the library, by giving readers such books as they ask for and then helping them in the choice of books, conducting them, say from the ordinary society novel to the historical novel, and then to the proofs and illustrations of the events or periods commemorated in the more readable of the historians. Multitudes of readers need only be put in this path to follow it.[8]

J. P. Quincy's essay was the most hostile to fiction. He gave grudging assent to the established view, quoting what he called "better American opinion" on the subject which "he is not concerned to dispute":

> There is a vast range of ephemeral literature, exciting and fascinating, apologetic of vice or confusing distinctions between plain right and wrong . . . responsible for an immense amount of the mental disease and moral irregularities . . . in modern society, and this is the kind of reading to which multitudes naturally take, which it is not the business of a town library to supply, although for a time it may be expedient to yield to its claims while awaiting the development of a more elevated taste.[9]

Thus the authors who discussed the matter of fiction in the 1876 report affirm the position stated by Ticknor in 1852. Heavy circulation of popular fiction, even "trash," is not inconsistent with the library's purpose, but essential to it. Such fiction is the starting point for the process of self-education.

In the same year the report appeared, however, a gentle objection to the taste-elevation theory was published in the new *Library Journal*. And before the end of the decade, it was apparent that many librarians did not accept the theory. The public library community was divided by controversy.

Despite the controversy, there were several points on which the parties were in agreement. It was generally agreed that some works deserved to be classified as high-quality fiction and ought to be owned by all public libraries. Included were the works of such authors as Hawthorne, Scott, Dickens, Thackeray, Eliot, and others of that stature. Only one public librarian refused to stock the works of such authors: William Kite, librarian of the Friends' Free Library of Germantown, Pennsylvania, excluded all novels. As late as 1892, there was no adult fiction in the Germantown library. But no public librarian of his time or any other adopted his view.

There was another point of general agreement: Public libraries should exclude immoral fiction. There was disagreement about which books were immoral, but the general principle was accepted.

G. W. M. Reynolds was one author whose novels many librarians condemned as immoral. Twenty out of thirty libraries responding to a survey by an ALA committee in 1881 excluded Reynold's novels.[10] Of the twenty-eight authors named in the survey instrument, none was so widely excluded as Reynolds. His books portrayed criminals and lowlifes and their horrible deeds "with a lighthearted suspension of moral judgment."[11] His reputation for sexy writing was based on passages like the following: "Maria wore a morning wrapper, which was as yet open at the breast; and her young and beautiful bosom, which the garment only half concealed, heaved with frequent sighs."[12]

There was also general agreement among librarians that dime novels did not belong in libraries. These were cheap adventure stories—often of train robbers, detectives, or cowboys—turned out by some writers at the rate of one a week. Some librarians thought them immoral; others thought them relatively innocuous, but so miserably low in literary quality as to be inadmissible. The audience for dime novels included young boys who were more freely allowed to use the public library as age restrictions were gradually loosened during the last quarter of the nineteenth century.

The fiction controversy, therefore, centered chiefly on the novels of authors not generally regarded as immoral, but as sensational, trivial, vulgar, sentimental, and inauthentic in their portrayals of the problems and predicaments of human beings and society. These were the authors about whose works librarians argued most. The ALA list of 1881 named several of them; as new authors came on the scene, they were incorporated into the controversy. They were the authors whose works were characterized in the 1876 report as "feeble, rudimentary, perhaps sentimental," as "silly reading" and "trash," but nevertheless indispensable if the process of taste elevation was to begin.

Two representatives of this class were E. D. E. N. Southworth (1819–1899) and Louisa de la Ramée (1839–1908). Southworth wrote forty-three novels; she is the best-selling woman novelist in American history; twenty-seven of her books were still in print in 1936.[13] Basically she wrote soap operas spiced with violence. They bore titles such as *The Fatal Marriage*, *Tried for Her Life*, and *The Bridal Eve*. The following critical assessment of Southworth was rendered in 1895:

She has perpetrated about fifty novels, devoted chiefly to the narration of various crimes and the contrasting of hideous villains with patterns of virtue. Her distortion of truth and fact is wonderful, and her sentimentality appalling. Nevertheless, her books continue to be devoured by a reading public which would doubtless be wiser and more sensible if it had never learned how to read.[14]

Critics and historians of popular literature love to give representative quotes from Southworth's novels. They give the flavor of her writing:

Infatuated youth! Could he have foreseen the long and terrible agony which that goddess-like being had been ordained to suffer, and which was soon to burst upon her imperial head, he would, in the ungovernable passion of his wild Italian nature, have struck her dead at his feet, and gladly died for having saved her from such unspeakable woe.[15]

Louisa de la Ramée, who wrote under the name Ouida, was considered a cut above Southworth; but some libraries would not provide her books. The following criticism was representative:

Her powerful and picturesque imagination runs riot in the delineation of extravagantly splendid and generally immoral nobles, contrasted with improbable peasants, who are endowed by nature with either phenomenal beauty or talent. No representation of any kind of life could be more ridiculously remote from truth. Nevertheless, there are single episodes and scenes in many of her books that are described in a rarely beautiful way, exciting enthusiasm for physical courage or touching deeply the emotions of pity for misfortune.[16]

The novels of Southworth and Ouida represented the type at issue in the fiction controversy, the type that experts writing in the 1876 report deemed necessary for public libraries.

The November 30, 1876, issue of *Library Journal* reflected skepticism about the taste-elevation theory. The *Journal* published a statement made by a Philadelphia librarian named John Edmands; it was made at the ALA conference of the previous month. Edmands said:

Without implying any disbelief in the tendency of the reading of even inferior novels to elevate the taste of readers, I have not yet seen any very definite proof of it, and I should be glad if anyone here could give some facts that would substantiate the assertion. I recall an instance where a person regularly took from the library two novels a week, and continued the practice for fifteen years, without ever asking for anything better.[17]

Edmands got little assurance. William Greenough, a trustee of the Boston Public Library, said that he had observed fiction circulation for twenty years and was satisfied "that the character of the reading improved."[18] Other comments were not responsive to Edmand's request for proof.

The doubts gently voiced by Edmands were soon voiced by others with less restraint. Late in 1877, a paper appeared in the *Library Journal* attacking F. B. Perkin's version of the taste-elevation theory in the 1876 report. The author of the paper was a British librarian, Peter Cowell. Cowell summarized his paper with the statement that "the theory of a regular upward progress of reading from lower-class novels to the higher departments of literature is rather of the nature of a fiction itself."[19] In late 1879, in an issue of *Library Journal* largely devoted to the question of fiction in libraries, Charles Francis Adams, a trustee of the Quincy, Massachusetts, Public Library, wrote: "That insipid or sentimental fiction amuses, I freely admit, but that it educates or leads to anything beyond itself, either in this world or the next, I utterly deny. On the contrary, it simply and certainly emasculates and destroys the intelligent reading power."[20] In the same issue, a remark by Samuel Green, librarian of the Worcester Public Library, suggested that disbelief was wide-spread. Green, who was still a believer, said: "The taste of many persons does improve. You smile as I make this assertion. It is becoming fashionable to sneer when the librarian says that the boy who begins with reading exciting books comes afterwards to enjoy a better class of literature."[21]

Over the next ten years, the taste-elevation theory lost ground. By 1893, it was a minority opinion. A survey conducted that year included a question on the theory. Of forty-five respondents, ten reported that they still believed in it; ten were doubtful; twenty-five rejected it.[22]

As belief in the taste-elevation theory declined in the years following 1876, the fiction controversy began. One party to the controversy advocated the exclusion of inferior popular fiction. The argument offered was simple. The library is an educational institution; popular fiction has no educational value; therefore it should be excluded. The other party advocated the inclusion of inferior popular fiction; but different factions of this party urged different arguments. One faction argued that recreation or entertainment has social value and should be part of the library's purpose. Another argued that the library is tax-supported and must yield to public demand. Another argued that inferior fiction brought people to the library where they were exposed to educational books and the influence of librarians. Still another faction consisted of the remnant who continued to believe in the taste-elevation theory. Some librarians belonged to more than one of those factions.

The effort to exclude popular fiction began as early as 1879. That year the trustees of the Burlington, Vermont, Public Library decided on a "wise innovation." The books of certain popular authors were withdrawn from the shelves.[23] About the same time, the Lawrence, Massachusetts, Public Library adopted the policy of not replacing "inferior" novels when they wore out.[24]

In 1881, the superintendent of schools in Boston called for the purging of the Boston Public Library. The offending books were not immoral, he said, but books

of the light, sensational kind serving to amuse an idle hour, but leaving the mind no better for the amusement. Such reading not only wastes time, but it injures the mental tone and destroys a taste which might otherwise be developed. . . . The only effectual remedy for the evil would seem to be to purge the library at once of all

objectionable matter, burn all the "trash" now on the shelves, and never allow any
more to be put there.[25]

The superintendent's view was quite in line with that of the committee
auditing the Boston Public Library's operations at that time:

The Lower Hall contains an excess of juvenile stories and poor novels, which, though
not immoral . . . must be considered bad reading. Their tendency, moreover, is to
develop a taste for similar and worse literature rather than that of a higher grade.
We are glad to understand . . . that efforts are making to turn the attention of readers
to more worthy objects; still we believe more energetic action would be advisable.[26]

More energetic action was being taken elsewhere. In 1882, the librarian
of the Cleveland Public Library told the ALA conference in Cincinnati of
his success "in getting rid of a popular but . . . useless class of literature."[27]
As the novels wore out, they were discarded and not replaced. The 1882
Report of the Portland, Maine, Public Library recommended "that all such
books as those of Southworth . . . Alger and some others be withdrawn from
circulation."[28]

Meanwhile, many librarians continued to purchase and circulate popular
fiction as usual. In the early years of the controversy, few librarians justified
the practice in print; but two who did so, Samuel Green and Charles Cutter,
were influential and highly respected. Both Green and Cutter were strong
advocates of the library's educational purpose, but both opposed the exclusion
of popular fiction. They urged two considerations: recreation is valuable;
and the library is tax-supported and must respond to public demand.

In addition, both Green and Cutter had other beliefs that made them more
tolerant of popular fiction. Green believed in the taste-elevation theory. Cutter believed that if people could be attracted to the library, the efforts of
librarians to improve reading preferences could attain considerable success.

Green stated his position in a speech at the first ALA conference in 1876:

Our libraries are established for the whole community. Their existence can only be
justified, and money raised by taxation for their support, when large portions of the
community receive benefit from them. . . . There is another consideration. . . . Popular
libraries are not established merely for instruction. It is meant that they should give
entertainment also. They are regarded as a means of keeping order in the community
by giving people a harmless source of recreation.

Green went on to say that librarians need to discriminate among novels, that
in the Worcester library

we do not leave any places on the shelves for the writings of Mrs. Southworth and
Mrs. Stephens. That is to say, we keep the supply of this class of books as low as
will be tolerated by the supporters of the library. . . . There must be some sensational

books in a public library. Citizens own the libraries, and they demand their presence. . . . Neither citizens nor city government will support a library generously that does not contain the books they and their families want.[29]

Cutter gave his view early in 1878 in an article written for the *Boston Daily Advertiser;* the article, reprinted in *Library Journal,* stated:

As the public library is for all the citizens, and not merely for the well-educated, the trustees may properly believe themselves justified in providing a kind of reading which is sought for by a large class; gives them pleasure; does them at least no harm . . . brings them a certain amount of intellectual profit . . . and finally, that attracts them to the library, where there is a chance that something better may get hold of them. . . . It is very well to say, these people must be made to prefer good reading; but how is it to be done? What power is to compel them? Certainly nothing can be effected by a policy that will begin by driving them off. The true way is to get them in the habit of frequenting the library, and then to raise by personal influence the character of the reading.[30]

In the early 1880s, the strongest published support for including popular fiction came from the popular press. The newspapers stressed the importance of recreation or amusement. The *Library Journal* reprinted several articles; the following were typical:

The common argument against novels in public libraries, that at the best they afford only harmless pleasure, and that the public money ought not to be spent in providing pleasures for the public, is not sound. . . . What government ever refused . . . to make provision for public parks, or for public amusement, such as fire-works or band playing? . . . Pleasure in itself is not only not ignoble, but it is certainly one, and not the least, among the objects of existence.[31]

The *Boston Sunday Herald,* in an article entitled "The Other Side," said of the public library: "It's purpose is not purely educational, as many seem to think. . . . It is, what its name implies, a great popular library, and is designed to give pleasure to the masses of the citizens, as well as to impart instruction."[32]

Another newspaper reminded librarians who would exclude popular fiction that:

there are a great many tired people in the world, a great many people whose lives are not very bright . . . a great many people with leisure too limited to allow of the cultivation of a fine and accurate taste, to whom the reading of a bright book of fiction, which doesn't tax their energies at all, is like a draught of cool water to a thirsty man. It takes the tangles out of their brains, lightens the load of care, rests them, and puts a little play of fancy into lives that are pretty well crowded with hard facts.[33]

Many librarians, apparently, were receptive to such arguments. In 1883, Mellen Chamberlain, Winsor's replacement at the Boston Public Library, gave a "Report on Fiction" at the ALA conference in Buffalo. He reported that fiction reading was "epidemic"; and speaking, no doubt, for many librarians who opposed the exclusion of fiction, Chamberlain said:

A public library is chiefly maintained by a levy on the persons and estates of the citizens, and controlled by trustees, dependent for their election and continuance in office upon the popular vote; and, in respect to these libraries, the number of which will increase indefinitely, we may as well make up our minds now, as we shall be obliged to sooner or later, that the books purchased for them will be mainly such as the public demand. We may wish otherwise; but it will not be otherwise. We may believe that the trustees have no right to expend the public money for the mere amusement of the people; but if the people think differently, trustees must yield to their wishes or leave.[34]

Chamberlain concluded his remarks by telling his colleagues that they could not enlighten the world and should not set themselves above the communities in which they worked.

William F. Poole spoke at the same conference. He was not so willing to acknowledge the imperative of public demand:

Our public libraries and our public schools are supported by the same constituencies, by the same methods of taxation, and for the same purpose; and that purpose is the education of the people. For no other object would a general tax for the support of public libraries be justifiable. If public libraries shall, in my day, cease to be educational institutions, and serve only to amuse the people and help them to while away an idle hour, I shall favor their abolition.[35]

In the remaining years of the decade, it is clear that many, and indeed probably most, librarians were providing the public with all the fiction it wanted. It is uncertain whether they did so in willing or grudging response to public demand, because of belief in the taste-elevation theory, or belief in the value of recreation. But there is little doubt about the fact. The advocates of exclusion who expressed their dismay testify to the fact. In 1884, J. N. Larned of the Young Men's Library in Buffalo called upon public librarians to exercise the "common verdicts of the literary world" and "sweep a mountain of rubbish from their shelves."[36] In 1887, Max Cohen, a librarian from New York City, told a meeting of the New York Library Club: "We are losing sight of the fact that the great mass of reading done by the people is devoted to novels and romances. Library statistics show that the amount of fiction circulated ranges in different libraries from sixty to eighty per cent, and reaches in some as high as eighty-seven. . . . Hosts of future American women are being intellectually matured on . . . unmitigated trash."[37]

In 1889, James M. Hubbard, formerly of the Boston Public Library, in an article published in the *North American Review*, gave his appraisal of the current situation. Public libraries were established, he said, "to promote the education and elevation of the people." But this has not happened. "Libraries are in no true sense of the words educators of the people. They are the haunt, in every place, of a few scholars and persons of leisure, but their chief work is to furnish amusement for the young." This has happened in spite of "strenuous efforts for some years past . . . to counteract this tendency."[38]

In September 1890, *Library Journal* published four short articles under the title "Fiction in Libraries." The editors evidently took care to solicit four different views. One author was a librarian named J. L. Schwartz. He had earlier gained some notoriety because of an article advising librarians as follows: "Don't try to force people to use what you think is best for them simply because you happen to like it yourself. Buy only what your customers want, then you won't have any dead stock."[39] In his 1890 article, Schwartz not unexpectedly advised librarians to collect all fiction not immoral.

The three other articles took different positions. W. A. Bardwell of the Brooklyn Public Library offered an old-fashioned plea for the taste-elevation theory. He knew of a boy who advanced from low adventure stories to *Ivanhoe* to a biography of King Richard. Another contributor was Samuel Green. He still favored "exciting stories"; but he believed librarians should make efforts to improve reading levels. He advised librarians not to buy questionable novels till they received "commendatory notices"; he recommended that librarians "regulate" novel reading through the use of lists designed to lead readers to higher levels, by assigning "pleasant and accomplished assistants" to help readers select books; and, Green said, "do not allow library users to change novels or stories oftener than twice a week."[40] Herbert Putnam of the Minneapolis Public Library represented the strict advocates of education: "Unless our public libraries draw the line absolutely at what they believe to be of educational value they will forfeit the confidence of the better minds in the community."[41]

In July 1893, an article appearing in *Library Journal* gave the misleading impression that the opponents of popular fiction were winning. Ellen M. Coe of the New York Free Circulating Library published results of a survey of seventy-five librarians on matters relating to fiction. Her assessment of the sixty replies was that "the ALA, voiced by the sixty gives forth no uncertain sound as to the necessity and duty of restricting the provision for fiction (novels, strictly so speaking) to the smallest possible quantity of the best quality." She was apparently led to her assessment by answers like the one received to question number ten: Do you "endeavor to check or restrain" fiction reading and direct it "into other channels?" Of forty-eight replies, twenty-eight were yes, twenty no.[42]

Later that year, Tessa Kelso, librarian of the Los Angeles Public Library, published a sharp attack on opponents of popular fiction, recreational reading, and recreation in general. She accused those opponents of hampering public library development and thwarting the library's most valuable contribution to society—that is, adding "to the fast-diminishing store of human pleasure." Librarians, Kelso said, had hurt their own cause "by constantly deprecating the reading of fiction or any literature that might be read for amusement. . . . This insistence against fiction has furnished a weapon to be used against the support of public libraries." The library, according to Kelso, could make an important contribution to solving the growing problems of urbanization which constitute a "new social danger" caused by "lack of relaxation," of opportunities for "intellectual improvement" and lack of amusement. Librarians should cease their wrongheaded opposition to recreation: "If the library did no more than become the recognized loafing center of a city, its existence on that basis would be warranted." Few, if any, librarians were stronger advocates of recreation than Kelso:

Parents, teachers and librarians are continually holding endless discussions as to how to curtail the reading of estimated trashy and flabby literature; but the question of what is to take its place as a recreation is left to solve itself. . . . Let the library meet the demand for the hundreds and thousands of volumes of this style of literature, with a proportionate number of sets of tennis, croquet, footballs, baseballs . . . and the whole paraphernalia of healthy, wholesome amusement.[43]

In 1894, it became more clear that professional support for the exclusion of popular fiction was dwindling. At the ALA conference at Lake Placid, five papers were presented in response to the following question: "Is a free public library justified in supplying to its readers books which are neither for instruction nor for the cultivation of taste; which are not books of knowledge, nor ideas, nor of good literature; which are books of entertainment only?"[44]

The first paper was read by Caroline H. Garland, librarian of the Dover Public Library. Her answer to the question was yes. Garland said that so many people wanted commonplace books because they were "merely commonplace people." They sought entertainment in music and painting as well as in books. And, Garland said, "just as I admit the right of existence for the merely entertaining in other branches of art, so I admit that right for fiction in a library. Otherwise, I think we would be insufferable prigs."[45]

The second speaker, Elizabeth Thurston of the Newton Free Library, was lukewarm in favor of entertainment. She recommended providing the best possible entertainment novels and trying to guide people to something better.

The third speaker, George Watson Cole of the Jersey City Public Library, subtitled his paper "A Plea for the Masses." He summarized his position as follows:

I favor the freest admission into our public libraries of all kinds of fiction except that which is positively impure or immoral. . . . It is a condition not a theory that confronts us. Say what we will, we cannot get rid of the facts as they exist. We are not called upon to apologize for the taste of the masses, which finds expression in the large percentage of fiction shown by our library statistics. The fact, unwelcome as it may be to the theorist, remains . . . that there exists a craving or demand which must be satisfied and which, if properly directed, will result in much good. If the public library is for the benefit of the general public . . . it must supply this demand, or the public will be perfectly justified in withholding its support.[46]

The fourth paper was by A. W. Whelpley, librarian of the Cincinnati Public Library. He thought that common novels were not as bad as some might say: "It has to be a remarkably shallow book that has not some good in it for someone. . . . What so large a part of the people in all great cities need, is something to entertain them, something to take them away from their own cares, and make them interested in other things than the petty matters of their everyday lives." He also believed that reading common novels "will lead to a want for literature of a higher order, other than fiction."[47]

The last speaker, Ellen Coe, appeared a little shocked. Only a year earlier she thought she had seen signs that librarians were turning against common novels. Coe said she was glad she did not write her paper before coming to the conference. Her paper, she said, was a reply "to all arguments pleading the adoption of any other than the highest standard in the selection of novels for public libraries, for any politic or other reason whatsoever."[48] She then made a less than compelling plea for the library's educational purpose.

The Lake Placid symposium of 1894 gave a true picture of the status of the fiction controversy. The advocates of popular fiction and recreation were the winners. Before the century ended, the controversy languished and died. Articles on one side or the other of the question appeared, but with decreasing frequency, adding nothing. The subject was thoroughly exhausted. The opponents of popular fiction and recreation had grown old and died, been won over, or been reduced to a negligible few.

In early 1902, an editorial in *Library Journal* remarked that "the fiction question, after some years of tranquillity, is again a subject of agitation and discussion."[49] The flare-up was the result of a "radical" proposal by Herbert Putnam, then Librarian of Congress, that public libraries buy no work of fiction until it was a year old. But the preceding years of tranquillity signified more than Putnam's proposal. The matter was settled.

By the mid–1890s the original theory of the public library, set forth in 1852 and reaffirmed in 1876, was extinct. The original theory was that the public library is an educational institution in essentially the same sense in which the public school is an educational institution. Popular novels lent in great numbers by the library were part of the educational program. Novel reading was the first step on the path of self-culture through books.

By the mid–1890s, most librarians no longer believed that popular novels were part of an educational program. Most librarians believed that popular novels provided recreation. Some people might be led by novels to prefer better books, but most would not; most people would use the library for recreation. Many librarians, like Tessa Kelso and George Watson Cole, were not troubled by this; providing recreation seemed like a valuable social service. Other librarians may have been troubled, but most of these also believed that nothing could be done. They accepted the judgment so often rendered that the library must respond to public demand.

For a while, in the mid–1890s, it appeared that discouragement might descend upon the public library community. It would not have been surprising. The institution that had once aspired to a high educational purpose had become, primarily, an agency of popular recreation. However one might try to inflate the importance of recreation, it was hard to assign it a value approaching that of education.

The tone of the discouragement was indicated and the reasons for it set forth in a speech that a leading librarian presented to the 1896 ALA convention in Cleveland. John Cotton Dana, librarian of the Denver Public Library and president of ALA, told the convention:

I sometimes fear my enthusiam for the free public library is born more of contagion than conviction. Consider the thing in some of its evident aspects. You have a building. . . . In it are stored a few thousand volumes, including of course, the best books of all time—which no one reads—and a generous per cent of fiction of the cheaper sort. . . . Of those who come to the delivery counter, if our friends tell the truth, sixty to eighty per cent rarely concern themselves . . . with anything outside of fiction. . . . And of this sixty to eighty per cent, a large portion—probably at least half—prefer to get, and generally do get, a novel of the cheaper kind. I am stating the case plainly. . . . Has it not often come sharply home to every one of you—the hopelessness of the task we assume to set ourselves, the triviality of the great mass of the free public library's educational work, the discouraging nature of the field, the pettiness, the awful pettiness, of results? . . . We are, to put bluntly, of very little weight in the community.[50]

Dana was not alone in his discouragement. A comment on his speech appearing in the new journal *Public Libraries* observed that librarians "cannot help but assent to the truth of most of the sentiments expressed."[51]

But discouragement never took root. It was swept away by a rush of optimism and high aspirations that swept over the public library community after 1894. Librarians discovered a great new mission for the public library in a changing society faced with immense problems, a mission even more grand and important than the original one.

NOTES

1. Edward G. Holley, *Raking the Historic Coals: The ALA Scrapbook of 1876* (Beta Phi Mu, 1967), 18.
2. William F. Poole, "The Organization and Management of Public Libraries,"

in U.S. Bureau of Education, *Public Libraries in the United States of America: Their History, Condition and Management, Special Report* (Washington: Government Printing Office, 1876), 477.

3. William I. Fletcher, "Public Libraries in Manufacturing Communities," in U.S. Bureau of Education, *Public Libraries in the United States of America*, 405.

4. J. P. Quincy, "Free Libraries," in U.S. Bureau of Education, *Public Libraries in the United States of America*, 395.

5. Poole, "The Organization and Management of Public Libraries," 479–80.

6. Fletcher, "Public Libraries in Manufacturing Communities," 410–11.

7. F. B. Perkins, "How to Make Town Libraries Successful," in U.S. Bureau of Education, *Public Libraries in the United States of America*, 420–22.

8. Justin Winsor, "Reading in Popular Libraries," in U.S. Bureau of Education, *Public Libraries in the United States of America*, 432.

9. Quincy, "Free Libraries," 395.

10. Esther Jane Carrier, *Fiction in Public Libraries: 1876–1900* (New York: Scarecrow Press, 1965), 268–69.

11. Dee Garrison, *Apostles of Culture: The Public Librarian and American Society, 1876–1920* (New York: Free Press, 1979), 84.

12. Garrison, *Apostles of Culture*, 84.

13. Garrison, *Apostles of Culture*, 81.

14. Augusta H. Leypoldt and George Iles, *List of Books for Girls and Women and Their Clubs* (Boston: Library Bureau, 1895), 33. Quoted in Carrier, *Fiction in Public Libraries*, 284.

15. "Review of *The Bridal Eve*, by Mrs. E. D. E. N. Southworth," *Critic* 1 (October 8, 1881): 276. Quoted in Carrier, *Fiction in Public Libraries*, 287.

16. Leypoldt and Iles, *List of Books for Girls and Women and Their Clubs*, 10. Quoted in Carrier, *Fiction in Public Libraries*, 301.

17. "Novel Reading," *Library Journal* 1 (November 30, 1876): 96.

18. Ibid., 100.

19. Peter Cowell, "On the Admission of Fiction in Free Public Libraries," *Library Journal* 2 (November-December 1877): 158.

20. Charles Francis Adams, "Fiction in Public Libraries and Educational Catalogues," *Library Journal* 4 (September-October 1879): 334.

21. S. S. Green, "Sensational Fiction in Public Libraries," *Library Journal* 4 (September-October 1879): 349.

22. Ellen M. Coe, "Fiction," *Library Journal* 18 (July 1893): 251.

23. Fletcher Free Library, "Report," *Library Journal* 6 (March 1881): 161.

24. Lawrence, Massachusetts, Public Library, "Report," *Library Journal* 6 (March 1881): 161.

25. E. M. Seaver, "Reply to James M. Hubbard," *Library Journal* 6 (March 1881): 45.

26. "Report of the Visiting Committee," *Library Journal* 6 (March 1881): 46–47.

27. I. L. Beardsley, "Fiction in Libraries," *Library Journal* 7 (July-August 1882): 176.

28. Portland, Maine, Public Library, "Report," *Library Journal* 7 (May 1882): 89.

29. "Novel Reading," *Library Journal* 1 (November 30, 1876): 99.

30. Charles A. Cutter, "The Public Library and Its Choice of Books," *Library Journal* 3 (April 1878): 73.

31. "Fiction and Public Libraries," *Worcester Daily Spy* (February 3, 1881), reprinted in *Library Journal* (February 1881): 28.

32. "The Other Side," *Boston Sunday Herald* (March 20, 1881), reprinted in *Library Journal* 6 (May 1881): 162.

33. "A Plea for Novels," *Boston Journal*, reprinted in *Library Journal* 7 (May 1882): 86.

34. Mellen Chamberlain, "Report on Fiction in Public Libraries," *Library Journal* 8 (September-October 1883): 209.

35. "Buffalo Conference Proceedings," *Library Journal* 8 (September-October 1883): 281.

36. J. N. Larned, "Public Libraries and Public Education," *Library Journal* 9 (January 1884): 10.

37. New York Library Club, "Discussion," *Library Journal* 12 (January-February 1887): 77.

38. James M. Hubbard, "Are Public Libraries Public Blessings?" *Library Journal* 14 (October 1889): 407.

39. Jacob L. Schwartz, "Business Methods in Libraries," *Library Journal* 13 (November 1888): 334.

40. "Fiction in Libraries," *Library Journal* 15 (September 1890): 263.

41. Ibid.

42. Ellen M. Coe, "Fiction," *Library Journal* 18 (July 1893): 250–51.

43. Tessa L. Kelso, "Some Economical Features of Public Libraries," *Library Journal* 18 (November 1893): 473–74.

44. "Common Novels in Public Libraries," *Library Journal* 19 (December 1894): 14.

45. Caroline H. Garland, "Common Novels in Public Libraries," *Library Journal* 19 (December 1894): 15.

46. George Watson Cole, "Fiction in Libraries: A Plea for the Masses," *Library Journal* 19 (December 1894): 21.

47. A. W. Whelpley, "Common Novels in Public Libraries," *Library Journal* 19 (December 1894): 21–22.

48. Ellen M. Coe, "Common Novels in Public Libraries," *Library Journal* 19 (December 1894): 23.

49. Editorial, *Library Journal* 27 (March 1902): 119.

50. J. C. Dana, "Hear the Other Side," *Library Journal* 21 (December 1896): 1, 3.

51. "Conference Report," *Public Libraries* 1 (October 1896): 219.

3

The Library Militant

1894–1920

In the 1890s, leaders of the public library community were aware that the country was changing. At the ALA meeting at Lake Placid in 1894, William H. Brett of the Cleveland Public Library discussed the changes:

The United States of 1894 is . . . a vastly different country from that of 1864. The reasons for this are manifold. The emancipation and enfranchisement of an enslaved race, the influx of a large foreign population, the settlement and development of the West, the concentration of business of all kinds into great establishments, the shifting of population from the abandoned farm and the depleting village to the congesting city, all conspire . . . to radically change the very texture of our national life.[1]

Public librarians believed that the changes created the opportunity for the public library to play a new, unique, and more important role in society. That was the theme of the president's address at the Lake Placid conference. The speaker was J. N. Larned of the Buffalo Public Library:

Eighteen years ago, the conception of the library militant, of the library as a moving force in the world, of the librarian as a missionary of literature was one which a few men only grasped. . . . Today such ideals are being realized in most corners of the American republic. The last generation, and the generations before the last were satisfied with the school as an agent of popular education. In our time we have brought the library to the help of the school, and the world is just opening its eyes to perceive the enormous value of the reinforcement that is gained from this new power. And the discovery has come none too soon; for a desperate need of more and stronger forces in the work of popular education is pressing on us.

Larned then referred to the new social conditions and the need for democracy to meet the test imposed by them. Popular ignorance was the great threat. It could not be met by the schools alone; and the newspapers were no help.

They were part of the problem. There was "action and reaction between what is ignorant and vulgar in the public and what is mercenary and unscrupulous in the press." This action and reaction "will go on until popular education from other sources puts an end to it." Fortunately, "there are other sources and foremost among them are the public libraries." Larned envisioned glorious achievement:

It is only the beginnings we have witnessed as yet. I am persuaded that the public library of the future will transcend our dreams in its penetrating influence. . . . Those of us who have faith in the future of democracy can only hold our faith fast by believing that the knowledge of the learned, the wisdom of the thoughtful, the conscience of the upright, will some day be common enough to prevail, always, over every factious folly and every mischievous movement that evil minds or ignorance can set astir. When that blessed time of victory shall have come, there will be many to share the glory of it; but none among them will rank rightly before those who have led and inspired the work of the public libraries.[2]

Two years later, Mary S. Cutler of the New York State Library School at Albany told the Pennsylvania Library Club that the 1894 speeches of Brett and Larned gave librarians the inspiration they had lacked. Referring to the previous eighteen years of ALA conferences, she said:

We are struck by the evidences of industry and earnestness. There are papers and discussions on libraries and schools, access to the shelves, bookbinding, systems of classification, cataloging rules. . . . But we sought in vain all along the years for the philosophic insight which should grasp the higher motive of our profession and connect it with the great struggles of modern life. After the Columbus year, in the clearer air of the mountain top, the word for which we were waiting came.[3]

Other public librarians exhibited the same great confidence that the library was equal to the challenge of the times. In 1897, Frederick M. Crunden of the St. Louis Public Library spoke to the ALA conference:

The public library is destined to play an important part, to exercise an incalculable influence in the solution of the social problems of today, and through this on the future of the nation and the race. The wisdom needed for this task is not to be obtained from schools or colleges, but from the higher education of mature minds—the masses of the people—which the public library alone can give.[4]

Contributing to the optimism of librarians was a theory, fashionable at the time, that universal forces of creative evolution, operating inexorably and beyond human control, were impelling civilization to higher levels. The public library, it seemed, was a tool of these creative forces. In 1901, Crunden wrote that human development is the lifting up of the great mass of humanity to an understanding of the significance of life, individual and social. For this work there is no such effective agency as the public library. What the varied activities of the world are unconsciously and indirectly doing, the public lilbrary is directing and consciously hastening. . . . This is the work of civilization. And we librarians should congratulate ourselves that we are thus engaged in the highest work that falls to the lot of man to do.[5]

During the last years of the old century and the early years of the new, public librarians were indeed inspired. They idealized the library as messianic, as an agency of national salvation. They saw themselves as missionaries enlivened by "the library spirit." There was constant insistence throughout the period that the library is an educational institution; but the educational task was transformed and glorified. No new formal theory of the public library was advanced; the educational task was transformed by enthusiasm and fervor. The new task was like that of a church. Missionaries are educators; but their real task is to go forth, evangelize, reform, and save.

The work of the public library manifested and was animated by "the library spirit," which Linda Eastman of the Cleveland Public Library compared to the spirit that built medieval cathedrals. That library spirit, "though as intangible and indefinable as its name indicates, is none the less the most real thing in the work, the vitalizing force."[6]

"The library spirit" was a favorite topic of editorials in *Public Libraries*. In 1896, the spirit was defined as a realization that "the opportunity of the age is in the grasp of library workers," that their mission is "second to none," and that they must provide "whole-hearted, sympathetic service."[7] An 1899 editorial reminded desk attendants that "all around them are great waves of that indefinable something called the library spirit, that in its sphere, is tireless in doing all the good it can, in the ways it can, to all the people it can."[8] A 1900 editorial spoke of the "beneficient influence of the library spirit in so many hamlets, villages, towns and cities," which, "by means of books, is making life brighter and happier for countless thousands."[9] In a 1901 editorial that reviewed progress of the previous year the writer said that activities of the year were "too great and too widespread to allow of an extended review and too well known to need it. But the conditions were never so hopeful as now, and the true library spirit is working its way gradually but surely in all directions."[10]

In an article entitled "The Library as an Inspirational Force," a leading librarian named Sam Walter Foss of the Sommerville, Massachusetts, Public Library presented his view of the library's role in more specific terms. Foss posed "test questions" for the library:

Is it grinding out a product of enlightened and symmetrical men and women? Is it transforming the community into intellectual, thoughtful, better equipped, more roundly developed citizens? Is it making life any ampler, is it making men any manlier, is it making the world any better? If there is a library that cannot answer these questions affirmatively . . . the taxpayers have a right to protest against its further existence.

Speaking of the librarian, Foss said, "Let him become the father confessor of minds in his town or city; the priest of the intellect, to whom all men shall bring all their mental problems, all their dubious enigmas of the brain." And of his predecessors: "I am sincerely glad that the old type of librarian is passing out—a man so dignified that children were afraid of him. . . . We want human men . . . men who can make themselves agreeable to men, women, children and dogs."[11]

At least some of the "old type" were fully as enthusiastic as Foss. William I. Fletcher, a contributor to the 1876 report, wrote in 1901 that by means of the public library "the community will be permeated with the intelligence, the aesthetic and spiritual culture of which it is the treasure house. Only by such means can the Twentieth Century be one of safe and steady progress toward the goal of a perfected and glorified civilization."[12]

In 1901, Henry Elmendorf, president of the New York State Library Association, addressed the members. His remarks indicated that the extravagance of librarians was sometimes observed with amusement by outsiders. Elmendorf nonetheless urged his audience to persevere:

We librarians have been accused of taking ourselves too seriously, and much wit and some wisdom has been expended in describing our true moral earnestness. But who will dare at this time particularly to cast discredit upon high ideals. We should raise high the banner which stands for our war against ignorance, selfishness and the spirit of lawlessness and unrest. . . . We will be most efficient when we become an organized army in our fight against evil and ignorance.[13]

That same year, Mary S. Cutler, by then Mrs. Fairchild, presented a case exemplifying the uplifting power of the library. Men in a carpentry shop had received in their pay envelopes an invitation to visit the library and "inspect the books on carpentry." One man said he got enough of carpentry at work, so while he was at the library

he read Adam Smith and Ricardo and Henry George and Mill and Sumner and Walker. His mental apprehension of what it all meant was very vague . . . but . . . he did get clearly the idea that a working man who is the master of a good trade has a better chance in the struggle for existence than one without. . . . As he kept on reading, the sense of his obligation to give his own child a good start in life grew upon him, and the man actually gave up his pipe for three years, until his task of giving the boy a trade was accomplished. This man's wife from her novel and her volume on domestic economy, got the notion of taking more pains with making her bread, of keeping her cellar clean, and of having a prettier parlor for her daughter's sake. The raising of ideals in standards of living is of great service in social development.[14]

In the early years of the new century, public librarians worked hard at their enormous task. A 1904 editorial entitled "The Library Spirit" congratulated them:

In almost no other profession is there to be found so much of the altruistic spirit as there is among librarians. Often with what seems insurmountable barriers before them, librarians as a class undertake their work and by the very force of their own faith in the ideals involved, compel the fruition of their efforts, and one of the most gratifying factors in the situation is the fact that the ideals expand as they are approached and lead on constantly to greater effort toward still greater results.[15]

Around 1905, any fair-minded observer of the public library had to agree that congratulations were deserved. The last fifteen years had been years of remarkable expansion and innovation. Libraries were springing up everywhere. In 1896, there were 971 public libraries owning a thousand volumes or more; by 1903, there were 2,283. Hundreds of libraries were built or improved at the turn of the century with the help of Andrew Carnegie, who at that time radically expanded his grant program. From 1886 to 1898, Carnegie promised money for library buildings to only nine communities. From 1899 through 1905, buildings were promised to 630 communities.[16]

Also in the years after 1890, state governments became more active in promoting library development. By 1900, state library commissions had been created in seventeen states. By 1910, there were thirty-five. Most commissions employed a library organizer who travelled around the state encouraging interest in libraries, helping communities that wished to establish one, training local librarians, and even selecting books. State library commissions also provided library service by means of travelling libraries. These were collections of one or two hundred books that were shipped around the state to small villages, summer resorts, or other out-of-the-way places. Residents of the area used the collection for sixty days and then sent it on to another place. In New York State any household lacking convenient access to a public library was entitled to a "house library." Ten books were sent from the state library to the nearest railway office. There was a charge of one dollar for freight.

City libraries also made efforts to provide easy access to books. Book collections were sent to public schools, police stations, fire-engine houses, and a variety of other places. In 1904, the Springfield, Massachusetts, Public Library reported that books could be obtained at 179 different locations in the city.

Another innovation of the years 1890–1905 was reference service. Before 1890, many librarians provided informal assistance to readers in much the same way that a well-read bookstore operator might assist customers. In 1886, William F. Poole surveyed 108 libraries. Librarians at fifty-three reported that they gave personal assistance to readers. The reference department and reference librarian were creations of the 1890s. In 1891, the phrase "reference work" first appeared in *Library Journal*. From 1896 on, reference work was included as a regular part of ALA conference programs. By the turn of the century, the reference department was established as a standard component of public library service. Reference work was represented as part of the library's educational program. The view of one leading librarian in 1904 was that "the reference work of the library gives the institution its greatest value and may be called the heart of the work. The very best talent obtainable should be placed in the reference room. . . . Here is where the real educative work is done."[17]

The most important innovation of the period was undoubtedly the development of children's work. Some libraries admitted children prior to 1890. But as late as 1894, according to a report given to the ALA conference that year, "seventy per cent of the libraries of the country had an age limit. . . . Children . . . under twelve or thirteen years of age could not enter a library building."[18] The situation changed quickly. In 1895, five libraries opened special children's rooms; six more were opened the following year. "And it is hardly too much to say that no public library of any size has been built since that time without provision for separate work for children."[19] A school for training children's librarians was started in 1900 in Pittsburgh.

The purpose for children's work was educational. In the children's department, said an 1899 article, "the library takes care to provide everything in its power for the education and development of children."[20] Some librarians expected a great deal. Melvil Dewey, in 1903, claimed that "recent investigations . . . have shown that the chief influence on the life of the child, and through him on the citizen of the future, came not from father, mother, teacher or school, but from the reading of childhood. The librarian . . . who guides more than any other force the reading of the community, therefore, holds in his hand the longest lever with which man has ever pried."[21]

Some city libraries did not wait for the children to come to them. They provided home libraries for children in poor neighborhoods. Typically, a volunteer from a charitable organization brought library books to a family's home. The charity or the library supplied a bookcase; the oldest child in the family was given the key. Friends of the children were invited to join a reading club. The books were left for three months and then exchanged for others. Reading club meetings included games, singing, sewing, trips to the country, trolley rides, and other activities.

During this period, public librarians also intensified efforts to encourage reading in cooperation with schools. In 1896, the National Education Association, at the urging of J. C. Dana, created a Library Department to investigate children's reading and promote cooperation between libraries and schools. Such cooperation was a matter of great concern to librarians during the missionary era.

The public library's effort on behalf of children was popular and seemed to have the desired effect. Taxpayers approved of service to children; and the service was heavily used. By 1908, in twenty cities with populations over 200,000 children's circulation was 38 percent of the total.[22]

The public library's missionary work also included immigrants. They were provided with books in their own languages; classes in English; lectures on food, clothing, consumer topics, health, American law, and so on. Immigrants were taught "to behave in the 'right way'—to remove their hats in the library building, to enter and exit through the correct doors, to be tidy in appearance, to be careful in handling public property, and to appreciate the responsibility of borrowing library books."[23] It was all part of teaching the American way of life.

Dedication and energy impelled the public library community to undertake activities and provide types of service that the first generation of librarians never imagined. In 1902, Herbert Putnam observed these developments and mildly suggested some consideration of them. The public library, he said, "is tending to become an institution of varied and complete function, with much material not strictly literary, and with ambition to render this attractive and useful by a variety of affirmative, even aggressive activities unknown in times past. The soundness of this tendency is not likely to be questioned by the public; it must be at least discussed by the librarian."[24]

But the war against evil and ignorance is won by aggressive activities, not by caution and propriety. In 1906, a woman with the impressive name Gratia Countryman, librarian of the Minneapolis Public Library, spoke for the zealous missionaries:

There is a sense of social obligation upon us. . . . We must help to realize the social righteousness. The library has the duty of being all things to all men. It is no longer simply a repository of books, it is . . . the cradle of democracy, filled with the democratic spirit, and it endeavors, as far as circumstances permit, to minister to all the needs of the community in which it dwells. The library stands for progress . . . but it chiefly means the raising of the moral, social and intellectual standards . . . and helping men and women to be more effective in every way. . . . The sooner we unveil the "gods of joy and good fellowship" in our libraries the better; the sooner we make the library a center for all the activities among us that make for social efficiency the better.[25]

Countryman acknowledged that there were limitations imposed by "the spirit of a library"; but for her and those of like mind, the limitations allowed great latitude.

The missionary movement continued unabated through the first decade of the twentieth century. Leaders of the public library community maintained their vision of the library militant. In 1909, Theresa West Elmendorf of the Buffalo Public Library gave a speech at state library association meetings in five states. The speech impressed its audiences and *Public Libraries* printed it in response to a general request. Elmendorf said that the United States was embarked on an experiment in self-government while, at the same time, the press was producing a huge flood of books and papers:

Shall not an institution that can select, organize, make available and, above all, disseminate the wisdom . . . needed . . . be the most powerful agent for the preservation and perfecting of democratic society that the world knows? . . . Should it not be the coadjutor of the family, the supplement of the school, the lay brother of the church, inspirer of law, bulwark of government?"[26]

Six years later, at the 1915 conference in Berkeley, ALA president Hiller C. Wellman provided a survey of library activities in progress and of services offered that revealed the extent of missionary work at its peak. Wellman's speech was a portrait of the public library striving to be all things to all men, hard at work to preserve and perfect democratic society:

It is becoming increasingly common for lectures, not simply on library or literary topics, but popular courses on all manner of subjects, to be provided by libraries and occasionally delivered by the librarians themselves. Here and there has been further adventuring in the field of direct instruction, with classes for children in science, for foreigners learning English, and even tentative correspondence courses. Exhibitions of all kinds are held . . . including not simply books, binding and prints, but paintings, rugs, porcelains and other objects of art, frequently natural history specimens, flower shows, occasionally industrial displays or commerical exhibits; and some libraries have installed permanent museums. Story-telling for children on an elaborate scale has not been unusual . . . sometimes conducted at playgrounds and other places where there is no distribution of books. . . . Work with children has been extended in manifold directions. We read here and there of games, dances, parties, particularly for the holidays, plays, aeroplane contests, athletic meets and other entertainments. . . . Adults too are not neglected. We are lending library halls freely for literary, educational, civic and charitable purposes . . . for social gatherings and entertainments as well. Here a library has established a social center for young women where "all the various arts and handicrafts can be taught free of charge" and there another has opened debates each week . . . with speakers chosen by the trustees. Photographs and prints of all kinds, music rolls, scores, lantern slides, phonograph records . . . historical and scientific specimens . . . stereoscopes, radiopticons, and lanterns . . . are often supplied. . . . In one or two cities branch libraries are employed in friendly visiting among the families of the neighborhood, or for social service work with factory girls. One library is reported to maintain close relations with the probation officer and juvenile court. . . . Elsewhere librarians are said to be aiding in social surveys. Not only is the reading of foreigners fostered, but their welfare in other ways is looked after. . . . Concert giving by libraries with victrolas is becoming not unusual; and now we are introducing moving picture shows. . . . It has been said . . . that librarians are peculiarly alert to social needs, and so eager to render all possible service, that once convinced of a real want in the community, they are prone to undertake to meet it.[27]

By 1915, however, the year of Wellman's speech, the missionary era was coming to an end. Although many public librarians, as Wellman indicated, were still zealous and active, the weariness, doubt, and disappointment that would eventually terminate the missionary era were well advanced.

Signs that the public library community was beginning to lose heart appeared around 1911. Public librarians had set out in the 1890s to lead in the victory of knowledge, wisdom, and goodness and to elevate and perfect American civilization. By 1911, they had been at the task for about fifteen years. As great as their accomplishments had been, the task undertaken seemed hardly begun. Doubt and discouragement germinated; the library spirit began to dissolve.

Early in 1911, an editorial in *Public Libraries* noted that "it is not always easy for those of the present time who are just entering library work to understand why the phrase 'library spirit' means so much to the older persons in library work. Its real flavor belongs to another period."[28]

Furthermore, the old-style speeches that once inspired librarians no longer had the same effect. Such speeches were still given; but by 1912 they were often merely boring. "What in their day," said a 1912 *Public Libraries* editorial, "and in their stimulating way were messages of import delivered by the prophets, have now become dull and platitudinous reiterations."[29]

Another editorial two years later, commenting on the work of some librarians of the past, exhibited the same sense of decline:

We are admonished not to "say that former days were better than these," and yet in justice it must be said that the spirit and extent of the work in earlier years were on a broader basis and developed a feeling of inter-relation and esprit de corps which is worthy of the highest admiration. . . . There are certain names connected with the earlier development of the work which bring a thrill of pleasure and appreciation, the counterpart of which seems sadly lacking in recent years.[30]

In 1913, Sarah Askew, a member of the New Jersey Library Commission, spoke to some New York librarians. Her remarks revealed some of the reasons for the gathering disenhancement. In a speech entitled "Library Heresies," she said that librarians may not be "the best fitted persons to undertake every job in town," that they may be neglecting their proper task when they "rush into playgrounds, civic work, women's clubs, teaching history to the schools, chair caning to the boys, sewing to the girls, manners to the tramps, politics to the politician and civics to the town council." She continued:

With fear and trembling, I announce my belief that if the free public library is the highest effort of democracy to crown itself, democracy doesn't know it. . . . The men haven't stopped saying, "Naw, I don't know where the library is, that's a woman's affair." . . . The laity still mix the American Library Association with the American Laundry Association; and while we librarians confer on Uplift, many folks go on reading nothing but the yellow journals.[31]

Askew's statements recognized troublesome facts that contributed to the discouragement of librarians. One fact was that the library was used by relatively few people; and few of the users were men. Early missionary fervor envisioned broad popularity for the library, but this never happened. To the missionaries, that signified failure. They had worked long and hard to attract people to the library; but the number of library users remained relatively small. Henry Legler, librarian of the Chicago Public Library wrote in 1917 of libraries serving sixty-nine cities with populations over 100,000: "It is entirely within the facts to say that not to exceed twenty per cent of the inhabitants of any given community use a public library regularly, and for a general average embracing the sixty-nine cities referred to, perhaps ten per cent would be a nearer approximation."[32] Those who had worked for years to make the public library a great popular institution were understandably discouraged.

Another fact recognized by Askew's speech was that the library was still mostly used for entertainment: Librarians "confer on Uplift"; people go on reading trash.

At the turn of the century, when the fiction controversy burned itself out, there was consensus in the public library community that recreation was socially valuable and that the library was justified in supplying popular fiction. At the same time, however, the missionary movement that was to achieve the triumph of knowledge, wisdom, and goodness could hardly have expected to achieve that triumph by providing amusement. The expectation of librarians had been voiced by Frederick Crunden in 1897: the library was to exercise "incalculable influence" by providing higher education for "the masses of the people." The high purpose of the missionary movement implied that the recreational role of the library would decline. An agency of popular recreation could not maintain claims to intellectual and spiritual leadership. To face the fact that the library continued to be used primarily for recreation was to relinquish such claims. Askew's speech called attention to the fact.

In 1915, *Library Journal* reprinted an article from *America*. Like Askew, the author, James J. Walsh, was unimpressed with the intellectual results of years of missionary work:

It takes only a passing examination of library conditions as they exist today to prove that the main purpose of the libraries is not to supply instruction, nor even food for thought, but to furnish amusement. . . . It is very evident that the main purpose of our libraries is to supply the very latest fiction and cheap magazines to those who come for them. . . . If it is understood that they are social bureaus for the provision of inexpensive amusement for people, especially for growing girls and for women who have not enough to do, then there is no doubt that they are fulfilling their purpose. If it is supposed, however, that they are really providing education . . . then their purpose is fulfilled to so slight a degree that it is barely worth talking about.[33]

Such charges were painful to librarians who had spent twenty years trying to make the library the nation's principal agency of enlightenment.

Librarians were also hurt and discouraged by public indifference and the failure of nonlibrarians to acknowledge an important social role for the library. The president of the New York State Library Association spoke of this at the association's 1916 meeting:

Our chief sorrow comes from the indifference of the community to our ministrations. . . . It is not cheering to reflect that most of the really intelligent praise of libraries has come from librarians. . . . It is disconcerting to note how seldom the library is referred to outside of library meetings, as a major force in social progress. We speak of the library world, but to the average social worker, it is only a tiny island barely visible above the horizon.[34]

By 1916, there was added cause for disillusionment. The terrible war in Europe was demonstrating that civilization was not evolving and advancing to ever higher levels. The unprecedented slaughter and horror smothered optimism. J. C. Dana probably spoke for many librarians when he said:

The war has shown us that we are quite uncivilized. . . . Even in this country the war spirit is so prevalent as to show that our work with the "best books," our children's libraries, our classics, our stories and all our other well-meaning exertions have not abated and probably never will abate man's natural ferocity. . . . Librarians cannot prevent the breakdown of civilization. What then can they do? . . . Perhaps our work is so trivial that no industrial or social changes and no revelations of our moral state, which the war tells us is very low, can afford any reasons for modifying it. At present that is my own view.[35]

By 1916, the missionary era was over. The faith that had created it had lost its vigor. The public library community was faced with the task of reconstructing the purpose for the institution in its charge. But there was hardly time for librarians to realize that the task faced them. In April 1917, the United States became involved in the war. The public library community, with enthusiasm reminiscent of earlier years, devoted itself to the war effort. The library became militant in a new sense.

The attention of the public library community turned quickly to the war effort. With characteristic willingness and energy, the professional community took on a huge job. The Library War Service Program organized by the ALA assumed the burden of providing library service to the armed forces at home and abroad. Thirty-six libraries were built in training camps with funds provided mostly by the Carnegie Corporation. Additional money was raised by fund drives; book donations were solicited; more than seven hundred librarians worked for the War Service Program, many of them overseas. About $6 million was expended on war service. Some seven million volumes were placed in camp libraries or distributed to servicemen. The War Service Program was a spectacular success.

The public library community was justly proud of its contribution, proud of the praise and expressions of gratitude received from military and political leaders and servicemen. Librarians were especially delighted to have served, at last, a vast community of men. Library periodicals featured exciting and inspiring stories of activities and events at camp libraries and of the benefits derived from books by different servicemen. The War Service Program gave the public library community an unprecedented experience of gratifying success.

At home in their communities, public librarians also worked to contribute to the war effort. Exhibits of guns and gas masks were found in libraries everywhere, along with war photographs and posters. Pacifist and pro-German books were removed from the shelves; pro-Allied propaganda was distributed. Red Cross workers were invited to make use of the library; and librarians read to them while they worked. Story hours were devoted to building patriotism.

Librarians actively assisted the Food Administration, a government bureau charged with food conservation. Libraries provided food exhibits, war menus, and pamphlets on war gardens and food substitutes. Librarians were also trained to answer questions about food, some of which were difficult to answer (Why should we eat corn meal so that wheat flour can be sent to the French and English? Why not send them the corn meal?).

Some librarians were excessively enthusiastic. A "roll of dishonor" listed the names of children who had not bought their quota of war stamps. A librarian at the Denver Public Library recommended supplying the Secret Service with the names and addresses of borrowers of certain technical and scientific books. The Wisconsin Library Commission told Wisconsin public libraries that material should not be added to the shelves unless it was unquestionably patriotic.

When the war ended in November 1918, the public library community was at a high point, possessed by an unaccustomed consciousness of success and high achievement. Librarians ended their war work determined to make their future work as satisfying and successful as that of the past twenty months.

A few months before the war ended, there was already anticipation that returning soldiers would provide new opportunities for libraries. Thousands of soldiers accustomed to library service during the war would continue to be faithful library users. "The things that gave them pleasure and profit while they wore the uniform are going to be much dearer to them from every standpoint than they ever were before."[36] The theme was often repeated. The War Service Program put "libraries on the map to a large part of our male population by teaching thousands of our men, unacquainted with libraries before the war, to use them."[37] "Every public library from Podunk to Wahoola will have to wake up to the demands of New America when these boys come home."[38]

Public librarians also believed that the postwar era would provide other opportunities for valuable service. These opportunities were not clearly identified; but they were much proclaimed. "We as librarians have the largest opportunities that have ever faced us. We more nearly have the public confidence than ever before. The time is ours if we can only grasp the possibilities, if we can only see things big enough."[39] "Reconstruction, that great new task with its many new implications . . . wants definition and application. The literature on its various phases is growing daily greater and more vital. Only the public library can attempt to keep up with it and make it available to the earnest seekers after light. Never before were the libraries so closely linked up with an actual public need; never before were their opportunities for service so great as they are today."[40]

Proclamations of the great opportunities were sometimes accompanied by negative appraisals of the prewar days. "On every hand I hear librarians saying, 'We must not lose this spirit—this momentum. . . . There must be no slackening, no slump, no dropping back.' . . . We must not assume that with the war our collective responsibility ends, and we may now go back to 1917 and take up the old threads where we left off."[41] A circular letter from the ALA Executive Board said: "We as librarians could never again be satisfied with prewar library conditions. We have seen bigger things; we have done bigger things. With our responsibility to the War and Navy Departments discharged, what then lies before us?"[42]

Some kind of great undertaking was called for; but what was it to be? It had to be ambitious to measure up to the great opportunities. But, at the same time, the disillusionment of the years before the war was still fresh. At the ALA meeting of 1919, a committee on an Enlarged Program for American Library Service was appointed. In September of that year, the executive board accepted the committee's report.

The committee recommended a program with several parts: completion of war service work, library extension, a project to develop standards for certifying librarians, a national survey of libraries, publishing and publicity programs, and other projects. The proposed Enlarged Program called for work that was described with reasonable clarity, work that might get done. The Enlarged Program, that is, did not call for enlightening the nation or perfecting democracy. The ambitiousness of the program was displayed mostly in the cost: $2 million, to be supplied by a fund-raising campaign.

In January 1920, the Enlarged Program was approved by a relatively small number of members present at a special ALA conference. However, trouble plagued the program from the start. Many librarians disapproved of some of its features; some thought it was a pet project of ALA office holders and were offended when objections were disregarded. Most of all, the money, so freely available during the war, was not forthcoming. It quickly became evident that the $2 million would never be raised. In October 1920, the Executive Board of ALA voted to terminate the program. It was quietly abandoned.

The failure of the Enlarged Program dampened postwar hope and enthusiasm. The public library community had to face the question the war had enabled it to ignore for a time: What should replace the defunct missionary movement? That movement had produced greatly increased numbers of libraries offering new forms of service. To what purpose should these libraries be dedicated? In 1921 and 1922, the public library community seemed listless and uncertain; it appeared that creativity and energy were exhausted. An editorial in *Library Journal* observed that "many have come to have a pessimistic notion that a 'library slump' is on"[43] Adding to the gloom was an announcement by the administrator of the Carnegie Corporation. He ended any remaining hope that grants to libraries, suspended during the war, would be resumed. It was a low point.

But low points are sometimes points for new beginnings. The public library community in 1922 was chastened, but not defeated. It was not long before past disappointments were forgotten as the public library community launched an ambitious new enterprise, adult education.

NOTES

1. William H. Brett, "The Present Problem," *Library Journal* 19 (December 1894): 5.

2. J. N. Larned, "President's Address," *Library Journal* 19 (December 1894): 1, 3–4.

3. Mary S. Cutler, "Two Fundamentals," *Library Journal* 21 (October 1896): 447.

4. Frederick M. Crunden, "What of the Future?" *Library Journal* 22 (October 1897): 9–10.

5. Frederick M. Cruden, "What the Public Library Is For," *Library Journal* 26 (March 1901): 141.

6. Linda Eastman, "The Library Spirit," *Public Libraries* 4 (October 1899): 342–44.

7. Editorial, *Public Libraries* 1 (July 1896): 90.

8. Editorial, *Public Libraries* 4 (December 1899): 449.

9. Editorial, *Public Libraries* 5 (December 1900): 428.

10. Editorial, *Public Libraries* 6 (January 1901): 12.

11. Sam Walter Foss, "The Library as an Inspirational Force," *Public Libraries* 4 (March 1899): 102–03.

12. William I. Fletcher, "The Public Library in the 20th Century," *Public Libraries* 6 (July 1901): 384.

13. New York State Library Association, "Proceedings," *Public Libraries* 6 (November 1901): 557–58.

14. Salome Cutler Fairchild, "The Function of the Library," *Public Libraries* 6 (November 1901): 528–29.

15. Editorial, *Public Libraries* 9 (December 1904): 494.

16. George S. Bobinski, *Carnegie Libraries: Their History and Impact on American Public Library Development* (Chicago: American Library Association, 1969), 14.

17. Mary Eileen Ahern, "Reference Work with the General Public," *Public Libraries* 9 (February 1904): 55.

18. Josephine A. Rathbone, "The Modern Library Movement," *Public Libraries* 13 (June 1908): 199.

19. Ibid.

20. Mary Conover, "What the Library Can Best Do for Children," *Public Libraries* 4 (July 1899): 320.

21. "Library Meetings," *Public Libraries* 8 (July 1903): 327.

22. Walter H. Kaiser, "Statistical Trends of Large Public Libraries," *Library Quarterly* 18 (October 1948): 278.

23. Rosemary Ruhig DuMont, *Reform and Reaction: The Big City Public Library in American Life* (Westport, Conn.: Greenwood Press, 1977), 101–02.

24. Herbert Putnam, "Some Points in the Growth of Libraries," *Public Libraries* 7 (December 1902): 465.

25. Gratia Countryman, "The Library as a Social Center," *Public Libraries* 11 (June 1906): 6.

26. Theresa West Elmendorf, "The Things That Matter," *Public Libraries* 14 (October 1909): 281.

27. Hiller C. Wellman, "The Library's Obligation," *Public Libraries* 20 (July 1915): 286–87.

28. Editorial, *Public Libraries* 16 (May 1911): 201.

29. Editorial, *Public Libraries* 17 (February 1912): 51.

30. Editorial, *Public Libraries* 19 (October 1914): 342–43.

31. Sarah B. Askew, "Library Heresies," *Public Libraries* 19 (May 1914): 194.

32. Henry E. Legler, "Advertising Problems of a Large City Library," *Public Libraries* 22 (July 1917): 280.

33. James J. Walsh, "What Our Libraries Should Supply," *America* (February 13, 1915): 430–32. Quoted in *Library Journal* 40 (April 1915): 297.

34. Frank K. Walter, "Rising or a Setting Sun," *Library Journal* 41 (November 1916): 795–96.

35. J. C. Dana, "What Next?" *Public Libraries* 21 (January 1916): 3.

36. Editorial, *Public Libraries* 23 (July 1918): 320.

37. Chalmers Hadley, "The Library War Service and Some Things It Has Taught," *ALA Bullentin* 13 (July 1919): 111.

38. Mrs. J. A. Thompson, "What the Library Will Mean to the Returning Soldier," *Public Libraries* 25 (February 1920): 62.

39. Charles H. Compton, "What Then?" *ALA Bulletin* 13 (March 1919): 11.

40. Editorial, *Public Libraries* 24 (February 1919): 47.

41. William W. Bishop, "President's Address," *ALA Bulletin* 13 (July 1919): 104.

42. Editorial, *Public Libraries* 25 (February 1920): 72.

43. Editorial, *Library Journal* 47 (February 1, 1922): 125.

4

Adult Education

1920–1948

In Western Europe and the United States after World War I, growing concern for the education of adults developed into a movement. A new term, *adult education*, became fashionable as the educational needs of adults no longer in school gained the attention of governments, professional educators, and other interested parties. The times seemed to demand such attention. The demobilization of armies, the extension of democratic grovernment, the enfranchisement of women, Western fear of communism, and the expectation of rapid technological advance made adult education seem a matter of obvious and urgent importance.

In the United States, as elsewhere, the adult education movement was new, but adult education activities were not. Reading and attendance at lectures and sermons were adult education activities older than the nation itself; and nineteenth-century America had produced several notable adult education institutions including the Lyceum, the Chautauqua, and the public library. Nevertheless, it seemed to many of those involved in the postwar movement that the problem of adult education was being addressed for the first time.

In 1919 and 1920, the public library community was occupied with the Enlarged Program. When it collapsed and postwar enthusiasm evaporated, the public community as a whole seemed immobilized. But some people within that community were aware that the adult education movement was under way and were working to make the public library a part of it.

The earliest efforts of librarians were concentrated on reading courses. The version of the Enlarged Program presented in June 1920 included an "adult self education" project calling for "the preparation of reading and study courses which may be pursued by any person who has access to a library or who can purchase books."[1] In April 1920, *Public Libraries* published an article by Carl H. Milam, director of the Enlarged Program. Milam wrote of hundreds of thousands of young men whose formal educations had been ended by the war who "might be stimulated to embark upon a reading course on a vocation, on civic questions or on history or literature." He wrote also of "millions of women, recently enfranchised," who wanted to study politics and government, and of older men and women "interested, as never before, in history, government, politics, sociology." Milam called for the "preparation and wide distribution" of reading courses.[2]

The efforts of Milam and others met with some success. ALA began to publish reading courses early in 1922. And, that same year, readers' advisory service was started at the Cleveland and Detroit public libraries. The service was designed to provide reading courses tailored to the individual. In the summer of 1923, the Chicago Public Library opened a "Readers' Bureau" offering the same service.

In September 1923, Carl B. Roden, librarian of the Chicago Public Library, spoke to the Illinois Library Association. He urged his audience to get involved in the adult education movement. Roden spoke contemptuously of the "present status" of libraries: "We stand today in the placid esteem of our communities somewhere between the tulip beds and monkey cages of the parks and the compulsory processes of the public schools." This situation, Roden continued, was "humiliating and thus provocative and challenging." He proposed a response to the challenge. "It is time," he said, "to give thought to the next step in librarianship if there is to be one. . . . It is my belief that the time is ripe for a new development in library service. I think it will be in the direction of placing greater emphasis upon service to the individual." The public library "is the one tax-supported institution that seems almost preordained to meet the rising call for leadership in adult education. . . . Here lies its great opportunity."[3] *Public Libraries* published Roden's speech with an editorial endorsement: "Not for a long time have librarians had so fine a presentation of the present situation, so clear an analysis of conditions, so direct a program for future progress." Roden "deserves the thanks of the profession."[4]

In January 1924, the *ALA Bulletin* announced that the program committee was planning to devote one general session of the upcoming conference to adult education; by the end of the year, public library participation in the adult education movement had begun in earnest.

A book published in June 1924 captured the attention of librarians and intensified their interest in the adult education movement. *The American Public Library and the Diffusion of Knowledge* was written by William S. Learned, an employee of the Carnegie Foundation for the Advancement of Teaching. Learned's argument was as follows: The diffusion of knowledge is of great importance for the advancement of civilization. Schools provide for the education of children; but the "adult community has been almost overlooked." There were three basic problems: The adult is not trained in the technique of "getting . . . ideas independently from books"; the adult has "no clear conception of a curriculum" leading to the understanding of a field of study; and "there is no institution available in which he feels properly at home."[5] Deplorable consequences result: "The daily losses in energy and material that result from sheer ignorance on the part of otherwise intelligent persons of how to avail themselves of the contents of books must be colossal beyond all calculation."[6] The solution to the problem, said Learned, "is simple and surprising": a community intelligence service with the necessary books and other materials; and specially trained personnel providing bibliographies, syllabi, outlines, and other aids to knowledge. Such an institution might also offer lectures, organize museums and art galleries, and show moving pictures. The proper location for this community intelligence service was the public library. Learned then described what he regarded as exemplary activities carried on and services provided by a number of libraries he had studied: the business library at Newark Public, service to immigrants at Seattle, service to teachers at Indianapolis, readers' advisory service at Chicago, and so on. Learned concluded as follows:

Could the new features that have just been described be combined in one city, the result would be an institution of astonishing power,—a geniune community university bringing intelligence systematically and persuasively to bear on all adult affairs. If duplicated from city to city and organized . . . for rural and semi-urban districts, it would immediately take its place as the chief instrument of our common intellectual and cultural progress. The true educational establishment of a town or city would in that case center in the public intelligence organization. . . . The elementary and secondary schools would be the subsidiary feeders for the greater institution.[7]

Learned's vision of a great role for the public library inspired many librarians to join in the adult education movement.

In the latter half of 1924, it became clear what part the library would play in the movement. In June, the Carnegie Corporation assembled the first conference on adult education. As a result of the conference, the Carnegie Corporation decided to carry out a series of studies of adult education. One study was to be conducted in cooperation with ALA; and in July, the Executive Board of ALA appointed a Commission on the Library and Adult Education to carry out that study. The study was not finished until 1926; but long before that time, the public library's adult education program was planned and set in motion.

On July 4, 1924, Judson T. Jennings, ALA president and librarian of the Seattle Public Library, gave a speech at the ALA conference. The speech, entitled "Sticking to Our Last," recommended an adult education program. "The library," Jennings said, "is logically ordained as the direct and primary agency of adult education." But the library's contribution must be consistent with its essential character. The library "deals primarily with books and reading—with print." Jennings rejected Learned's vision of the public library as a community intelligence service. Lectures, museums, art galleries and moving picture exhibitions were out of place; the library existed to provide books and promote reading. Jennings recommended two types of adult education service: indirect and direct. By indirect, he meant service to other organizations engaged in adult education. By direct, he meant readers' advisory service, the publication of reading courses, and projects to increase the availability of books "that are interesting and readable to the average man."[8] Before the conference ended, the Executive Board appointed Jennings chairman of the Commission on the Library and Adult Education. His proposals set the agenda for the coming years.

Under Jennings's leadership, the commission set out to realize his program. In May 1925, the commission, in cooperation with the ALA Editorial Committee, published the first item of a series of reading courses. The series, entitled "Reading with a Purpose," consisted of short pamphlets, each providing a concise essay recommending a given topic and a list of eight to twelve related books. The subjects include salesmanship, advertising, home economics, and investing; but the great majority of the pamphlets are devoted to the liberal arts. A total of sixty-seven titles was published before the series came to an end in 1933; about 850,000 were sold.

In accordance with another of Jennings's recommendations, the commission in July 1925 appointed a Subcommittee on Readable Books. The subcommittee was to "investigate the possibility of encouraging the production of more books of educational value, so written as to interest and be understood by men and women of limited knowledge." The subcommittee was also to prepare a statement indicating the need for readable books and describing their characteristics, to select subjects of the most immediate importance, and "to collect . . . examples of the sort of books that ought to be published."[9] Over the next several years, the subcommittee published lists of readable books and worked with publishers willing to produce such books. It also conducted studies of readability and cooperated with those performed at the University of Chicago and Columbia University.

The Commission on the Library and Adult Education took another important step in 1925. In November, the commission issued the first number in a series of bulletins entitled "Adult Education and the Library." This publication, which was issued until 1931, described adult education activities in progress at various libraries, promoted cooperation between libraries and other agencies, and kept librarians in touch with the work of the commission. The primary emphasis of the publication was on readers' advisory service.

In 1926, the commission issued its report with recommendations. They echo Jennings's proposals of two years earlier: provide readers' advisory service, provide information on local opportunities for adult education offered by other agencies, and provide materials to other agencies. The report also recommended action to improve the supply of qualified readers' advisers and readable books as well as the appointment by ALA of a permanent Board on the Library and Adult Education. The board was appointed in October 1926.

Through the middle of the 1930s, adult education in the public library was primarily identified with the work of the readers' adviser. The readers' adviser was the "embodiment of library adult education, with the planned reading program as its major service." Service to groups was provided "largely to encourage their use of the advisory service."[10] Librarians thus had a well-defined and distinctive role in the adult education movement.

The readers' adviser sat at a desk in the main circulation area or in an open-shelf reading room. The service began with an interview. A record kept by the adviser bore the name and address of the reader, the title of the course the reader was following, and an estimate of the reader's ability to read. The reader was asked to come to the adviser's desk whenever he returned a book or checked one out, a process that enabled the adviser to keep in touch with the reader's progress. If a reader failed to appear for a long while, a postcard or telephone call was in order. The adviser asked if the readings were in any way unsatisfactory, offered to revise the list, or offered "an extension of time." The reader, however, was not "pressed to report or to continue."[11]

Reading lists prepared by advisers usually consisted of about six books, though longer lists were not uncommon. Sometimes the adviser provided a standard printed list; but advisers were warned against the temptation to provide standard lists in order to save time and effort. "What really distinguishes readers' advisory service from ordinary library lending service is that it is individualized, personalized and painstaking."[12] Before including books on a list, the adviser "should have scanned them thoroughly and read enough here and there in each book to be fairly sure it meets his applicant's needs and reading ability."[13] To improve the adviser's ability to give good service, his "schedule should include a few hours each day for reading. . . . Study is as much a part of the teacher's job as teaching . . . and this is perhaps even more true of the readers' adviser who must range over an even wider territory in his knowledge than the teacher of a specific few subjects."[14]

Reader's advisory service as conceived by its strong advocates was well beyond the resources of the vast majority of public libraries. J. C. Dana pointed out the limitations in 1928:

No library has a staff large enough to spare more than a few minutes each day to the special demands of each of a few inquirers. To do what the shibboleth "Adult Education," as we are now interpreting it, asks us to do, that is, to act as guides and teachers to all the adults we can persuade to come and ask us what they should read, and how, and to quiz them on their progress and advise them from day to day—all that is quite impossible. Libraries have not now and never will have an income which will suffice to do it.[15]

The high cost of readers' advisory service undoubtedly explains why it was never widely offered in spite of all that was done to promote it in the late 1920s and early 1930s. In 1928, the service was offered by twenty-five libraries; in 1935, it was offered by only forty-four.[16]

Whether readers' advisory service was worth what it cost is open to question. There is little evidence on which to base a judgment; but a New York Public Library investigation of 1,250 persons who received lists over a seven-year period provides some indication. Over the seven-year period, the median number of books on the lists given to readers ranges from nine to twelve. The median number of listed books that were read is the same for all of the seven years: three.[17]

After 1935, professional opinion turned against readers' advisory service. For years, critics had been saying that the public library's contribution to adult education was too much identified with that service. For years, critics had been complaining of the cost. After 1935, the criticism, given added weight by the depression, took effect. Hard times had added many unemployed to the ranks of library users and had reduced library budgets as well. Expensive service to a few was hard to justify.

The depression hit libraries hardest in 1933 and 1934.[18] In 1934, an ALA committee on library revenues reported that "in large sections of the United States, the general property tax, for more than a century the main support of schools and libraries, has completely broken down."[19]

In 1933, ALA attempted to help hard-pressed libraries maintain minimally adequate levels of financial support by adopting a set of "Standards for Public Libraries." The standards were very general and brief; they occupied but two pages in an issue of the *ALA Bulletin*. They were noteworthy, however, because they were preceded by a statement of purpose, the first ever issued by the national organization. The statement read

The public library is maintained by a democratic society in order that every man, woman, and child may have the means of self-education and recreational reading. The library provides materials for education and advice in their use. It diffuses information and ideas necessary to the present welfare and future advancement of a community. It strengthens and extends appreciation of the cultural and spiritual values of life. It offers opportunities for constructive use of the new leisure. It serves all ages and classes.[20]

The following year, a more ambitious attempt to find financial help for libraries led to an expanded and more forceful statement of purpose. It was formulated in conjunction with a national plan designed to secure state and federal assistance for libraries. National planning in accordance with the example set by the federal government was widely advocated and practiced at the time. Planning seemed to offer the best hope for alleviating the distress wrought by the depression.

In January 1934, the ALA Executive Board appointed a planning committee. "A National Plan for Libraries" was completed quickly and approved in December 1934. The plan called for

federation and coordination of public libraries in large systems. . . . Assumption of responsibility by the state for public library service to all people in the state. State appropriations to supplement local library funds or to provide a minimum library program. A federal library agency to provide nationwide leadership in the library movement. Federal aid to equalize library facilities in the several states. . . . Coordination of all library resources and services in the interest of adult education, scholarship and research.[21]

The expectations of librarians were high. The ALA Council adopted a resolution calling for fifty to $100 million a year in federal aid.

The national plan necessarily included a statement of purpose; it set forth the benefits that society receives from public libraries. The statement was given in a section of the plan entitled "Library Objectives":

The objectives of a library are to asssemble and preserve books and related materials in organized collections and, through stimulation and guidance, to promote their use to the end that children, young people, men and women may have opportunity and encouragement:

—to educate themselves continuously;

—to aid in the advancement of knowledge;

—to improve their capacity for appreciation and production in cultural fields;

—to improve their ability to participate usefully in activities in which they are involved as citizens;

—to equip themselves, and keep themselves equipped, for efficient activity in useful occupations and practical affairs;

—to keep abreast of progress in the sciences and other fields of knowledge;

—to maintain the precious heritage of freedom of expression and a constructively critical attitude toward all public issues;

—to make such use of leisure time as will promote personal happiness and social well-being.[22]

The statement assigned a high educational purpose to the public library and asserted it with confidence.

As the latter half of the 1930s began, the public library community faced a problem in addition to the financial one posed by the depression. The decline of professional enthusiasm and support for readers' advisory service made it necessary to develop a different approach to adult education. The preferred alternative was "diffusion" of the responsibility for adult education throughout the library. The identification of adult education service with readers' advisory service should end. "Adult education purposes" were to permeate book selection, program planning, publicity, reference work, even cataloging and classification.[23] Progressive librarians sought to establish the "identification of adult education service and general library service."[24] Though the term readers' adviser remained in use, the original form of the service gradually became extinct.

In 1938, a small book was published that provided an analysis and appraisal of adult education in the public library. The book was *The Public Library— A People's University* by Alvin Johnson, a highly respected social scientist, and an able and veteran observer of public libraries. He had prepared a report on Carnegie Libraries for the Carnegie Corporation before that body announced its decision to end its program of grants for library buildings. *The Public Library—A People's University* was written at the request of the American Association for Adult Education and was financed by a grant from the Carnegie Corporation.

Johnson acknowledged that "the adult educational undertakings of the public libraries are in the aggregate impressive"; but, he said, "the work is only in its initial stage. No library has come anywhere near developing the possibilities within its easy reach."[25] Johnson believed that the public library's adult education potential was unrealized because most librarians were not that interested. Most librarians, he said, were "custodians and administrators of books," more concerned with circulation than with education. "If adult educational work will increase the circulation of books, at the same time raising the quality of the circulation, all librarians will regard this as related to their proper function. But if adult education should involve changes in operation that resulted in a reduction of circulation, most librarians would regard this with misgivings."[26] Librarians thus practiced, Johnson called "pure librarianship." For the practitioners, adult education was "only an incidental, perhaps minor, objective."[27] Their chief concern was promoting books and reading, whether educational or not, in order to achieve maximum circulation.

Johnson was not impressed with the educational effectiveness of the public library's main adult education efforts of the previous fifteen years. Most reading lists, he said, were designed to stimulate reader interest and promote reading. He did not condemn such lists, but denied that they were educational; they were tools of pure librarianship. Johnson viewed readers' advisory service as a serious educational effort, but one in need of improvement. Better trained and better paid advisers were especially necessary. It is not clear whether Johnson believed that readers' advisory service could have much educational impact. In one place he said that "society can make something important" of the service "if it will pay the price."[28] But in another place, he said that only "the rare individual" can educate himself through courses of solitary reading.[29] Concerning the public library's other major effort of

the previous fifteen years,—the discovery and provision of readable books—
Johnson had nothing to say.

Johnson believed that the public library ought to make an important contribution to American society. Democratic civilization depended on education, especially adult education. "Without an intellectually active citizenry
there is scant hope for real democracy and an improving civilization. . . . The
essential role of the public library in our democratic system is therefore
cardinal."[30]

Johnson believed that adult education was best carried on in "voluntary
organizations for study and discussion." His "ideal" was a "vigorous, independent adult educational organization, consisting of forums, debating societies, parents' associations, child study associations, reading clubs, literary
teas, voters' associations and the like all drawn together into a local adult
educational organization."[31] Such organizations required leadership if they
were to survive and sustain their vitality; and "it is difficult to see where
such leadership can come from except from the public library."[32] The library
had the requisites of leadership, a supply of books, and many facilities and
branches. If the public library could overcome certain obstacles, it might
assume "its rightful place as leader in the movement for adult education."[33]

Johnson identified four obstacles. First, libraries wasted money on books
that provide mere entertainment. A reader who wanted such books should
pay for them himself "as he pays for movies and other harmless pastimes."[34]
A second and "graver obstacle is the difficulty in finding the right kind of
books." The right kind were readable, sound, small, and inexpensive. Librarians could not rely on conventional sources for such books. "If the libraries are to play their proper part in adult education, they will probably
have to get out books of their own, prepared for their own needs."[35] The
third and "greatest obstacle . . . is the inadequacy of personnel." Too many
librarians were indifferent to adult education; library education prepared
them for pure librarianship. Library schools should provide training "in the
educational meaning of books and in the organization of educational
groups."[36] The fourth obstacle was lack of money. More money was needed
for additional and better personnel and to support the writing and publication
of the right kind of books. Some money might be saved by cutting back on
the purchase and circulation of "second-rate books"; but even if that were
done, more money would still be necessary.[37]

In the concluding paragraph of the book, Johnson praised the public library
and the professional community. He called the public library a "remarkable
achievement . . . one of the outstanding American contributions to civilization." Many librarians, he said were "able and devoted leaders, men and
women of outstanding personality whose work will live beyond them."[38]
Johnson was far from being a hostile critic. Many passages in the book praised
the work of libraries and librarians. He even had a good word to say about

pure librarianship. It had made librarians catholic in outlook, broad-minded, and averse to censorship. His final sentence looked forward to the time when the public library "shall make itself over into a people's university, sound bulwark of a democratic state."[39]

Johnson's book was widely read and much discussed by librarians; but his major recommendations were virtually ignored. There was little support in the public library community for his proposal that the public library take leadership in the organization of educational groups and even less support for his proposal that libraries undertake to supply the right kind of books. Librarians were gratified and inspired by Johnson's vision of the library as a people's university; but the steps he proposed appeared too radical. While many librarians stood with Johnson on the importance of the public library as an agency of adult education, the consensus was that the job could best be done by improving the quality of book collections and by placing greater emphasis on service to groups. That emphasis, however, did not require the library to undertake the organization and leadership of such groups.

As the 1930s drew to a close, events in the world at large rearranged the public library's adult education agenda. Nazi Germany invaded its neighbors and revealed itself to be not only a political and military threat but a dangerous enemy to democratic civilization. The public library community focused its attention on responding to the danger posed by totalitarianism. A statement sent by the Oakland, California, library board to the city manager typified the response of the public library community:

At this time, when the very foundations of government and of society are being shaken throughout the entire world, the fate of our democracy and of our civilization depends as never before upon the clear thinking and sane judgment of our people. In determining the final issue, the things of the intellect and of the spirit will be factors of at least equal importance with the material things of life. The support of libraries, "the universities of the people," is now justified as never before. . . . It is, therefore, with full and deep conviction of the high civic and social values of the services offered by the institutions we direct that we propose and recommend the adoption of this budget.[40]

When the low countries and France were overrun in the spring of 1940, the United States government accelerated preparations for war, creating the National Defense Program. In October, the ALA Executive Board appointed a Committee on National Defense Activities and Libraries. In December, the ALA Council issued a statement on "National Defense and the Library": "The wars now being waged are not merely against nations and races. They have as their aim the destruction of ideas as well, even in those countries not engaged in military combat. The freedoms and principles which represent the highest achievements of civilized society are menaced, from abroad and at home. Libraries are inevitably involved in this war of ideas."[41]

In April 1941, John Chancellor, the ALA adult education specialist, pro-

posed a fifteen-point program for "adult education in the present emergency."
Chancellor urged that libraries

help to keep alive truth and reason in the face of propaganda and emotionalism. Help
to keep alive the spirit of tolerance, understanding and good will. . . . Help to keep
alive and strengthen an intelligent loyalty to democracy. Help to develop the morale
and character essential in a national emergency. Help to keep alive the spirit of play
and recreation. . . . Help to develop a suitable program concerning military training
and service.[42]

Additional points were concerned with physical fitness, youth guidance, civil
rights and vocational training.

Many libraries sought to contribute to the national defense effort. Bookmobiles were sent to defense plants; special efforts were made to provide
technical materials for defense workers; one public library opened a branch
at a shipyard; public libraries near army camps offered soldiers special rooms
furnished with materials for letter writing; many libraries ran or joined in
book drives; reading lists and discussion groups featured national defense
topics.

While the National Defense Program was proceeding in 1941, there still
seemed a chance that the United States would not become involved in the
war. On that chance, the federal government encouraged planning for the
"Post-Defense" era. In June 1941, the ALA Executive Board created a Post-
Defense Planning Committee. Its work had hardly begun when Pearl Harbor
was attacked.

Public libraries were immediately called upon to assist the war effort. The
first page of the *ALA Bulletin* for January 1942 carried a proclamation by
President Roosevelt declaring that

Libraries are directly and immediately involved in the conflict which divides our
world, and for two reasons: first, because they are essential to the functioning of a
democratic society; second, because the contemporary conflict touches the integrity
of scholarship, the freedom of the mind, and even the survival of culture, and libraries
are the great tools of scholarship, the great repositories of culture, and the great
symbols of the freedom of the mind.[43]

On the page following the president's proclamation was a statement adopted
by the ALA Council on December 29, 1941. It called on every library to
"organize its services and expenditures without delay to meet the necessities
of a nation at war. Each library activity must stand a triple scrutiny. Will
it contribute to victory? Will it help to make a better America? Will it help
to make a better world? Whatever fails to meet this test must yield to things
more urgent."[44]

Librarians took up war work with great energy and enthusiasm. On January 12, 1942, a nationwide Victory Book Campaign was launched; about

18.5 million books were eventually collected. War Information Centers were set up in public libraries all over the country. The centers maintained bulletin boards for official announcements and war news; distributed publications of the War Department, Office of Civilian Defense, and other agencies; and answered questions concerning air raid precautions, bombs and poison gas, rescue work, first aid, nutrition, victory gardens, draft boards, rationing, conservation, health, and other matters. The Cleveland Public Library's War Information Center reported answering such questions as "what is the formula for blackout paint; who makes air raid shelters; how will sugar rationing be organized; is there any use for tin foil?"[45]

Beginning in May 1942, *Library Journal* published a regular feature entitled "Libraries and the War Program" in which libraries described their war work. It consisted mostly of posters, exhibits, displays, book lists, and materials and services for servicemen, military installations, and industry. The Des Moines Public Library set up a booth for recruiting merchant seamen; Wichita City, Kansas, hired a driver to bring bookmobile service to nearby aircraft factories. A few reports described library work being done in "relocation centers" where Japanese-Americans were imprisoned.

During 1942, issues of the *ALA Bulletin* featured inspirational pieces by public figures such as Elmer Davis, Raymond Gram Swing, and Nelson Rockefeller who urged the importance of librarians in the war effort. Librarians, said one of these essays, "are combatants from this time on in all countries where free libraries and a free culture still exist. . . . Librarians . . . are continually concerned with the problem of directing their readers to the materials which their readers require. In the present war as never before this duty of librarians assumes a first and pressing importance and librarians in consequence carry a responsibility such as they have never carried in our history."[46] Catalogers, like other librarians, answered to call to duty: "This time of testing presents to us as catalogers an unexampled opportunity to prove ourselves alert, flexible, and full of vitality. It is up to catalogers to lead the way."[47]

Not everyone was enthusiastic about the public library's war work. John Chancellor, the ALA's adult education expert, accused librarians of neglecting important educational tasks while going about their war work which "can make only a very slight and secondary contribution."[48] Chancellor resigned his position in the spring of 1942. Few librarians agreed with Chancellor however. The country seemed threatened. Everyone was being called on to help win the war. Business as usual seemed unthinkable.

Even before the first year of the war ended, however, librarians began to divide their attention between war work and another matter of vital concern, the problem of postwar reconstruction.

From the time the war became world-wide in December 1941, there was a general belief among Americans that the war signalled the end of an era, that the postwar world would be a new world. Planning for this new world began in the earliest days of American participation in the war; and librarians were involved in this planning from the outset. In December 1941, the Post-Defense Planning Committee for public libraries was renamed the Post-War Planning Committee. Early in 1942, the committee, at the request of the National Resources Planning Board, began work on *Post-War Standards for Public Libraries.* The standards were ready by June 1942 and were published by ALA in July 1943.

The introduction to the standards opened with a general statement about the library's postwar mission:

The impact of the present national emergency and contemplation of the inevitable difficulties of the post-war reconstruction period have awakened the American people to a determination to help make a better world in which to live. This new world must be *for* and *made by* the people. To achieve these ends, the agencies for the enlightenment of the people must be prepared for enlarged responsibilities. One of these agencies is the public library.

The introduction then characterized the particular contribution of the public library to American society:

It provides the means of self-education for all people in the community. It is a source of information on nearly every subject. It furnishes good reading for pleasure. It stimulates study and research, and helps to make possible many literary and scholarly achievements. It is basic to the education and continuous re-education of the American people as citizens, workers, and as civilized human beings. It plays a significant role in making democracy work by helping citizens to be enlightened participants in public affairs. It has come to be recognized as an essential part of our social and educational equipment.[49]

After the introduction, in a chapter entitled "Public Library Objectives," the standards restated the objectives (quoted earlier in this chapter) that were given in the national plan of 1934 and repeated when the national plan was revised in 1939. After listing the objectives, the authors of the standards cautioned librarians against "the dangers of too great diffusion of effort." Librarians should select "functions which are most useful in a democratic society and which the library is most fitted to perform." The authors then recommended "strategic areas for the concentration of public library effort": adult education, which was "perhaps the most important," vocational education, parent education, and service to young people and children.[50] The succeeding eight chapters presented standards for certain forms of service, for government and administration, finances, buildings, the book collection, personnel, and technical processes. Having completed the standards, the Post-War Planning Committee went to work on its other projects: an evaluation of public library service and a national plan for postwar public library service.

By the end of 1943, the public library community was primarily occupied with problems of postwar "demobilization and reconstruction." The *ALA Bulletin* dropped its regular feature, "Library War Service," after the December 1943 issue. Succeeding issues looked to the future. In February 1944, Carleton B. Joeckel, chairman of the Post-War Planning Committee, advised librarians that "the end of World War II will be the greatest punctuation point in modern history. . . . The library of the future must be ruthless in ridding itself of outmoded methods and unessential activities. Likewise it must be intelligently visionary in developing new fields and kinds of service."[51] Another article in the same issue outlined the scale of the postwar planning task. Librarians must plan "to help in the war worker's readjustment," to help solve psychological problems of "servicemen and war workers . . . of older men who have lost jobs and of boys and girls who left school to enter the armed forces or war industries. . . . Librarians need to help in planning for the wise use of new leisure and for the sound acceptance of the responsibilities of citizenship and of home and family life."[52]

Two months later, the *Bulletin* published "Demobilization and the Library: A Manifesto":

Millions of men and women will be discharged from the armed forces and war industries. They will have had new experiences, seen new places, acquired new skills, developed new interests. Some will be disabled. . . . Some will need physical rehabilitation. Most will seek employment. Many will want vocational training, general or professional education. All will have to reorient themselves to family and community life, to new economic conditions, and to new civic responsibilities. . . . Every public library should establish specially organized facilities equipped and staffed to meet this challenging opportunity.

The manifesto called for the establishment of "information service" to supply information on agencies serving veterans and war workers, on job opportunities, personal development, family adjustment, social and civic obligations, and psychological problems. The manifesto also called for increased and extended "educational service" to respond to "the inevitable expansion of interest in self-education," and called for a program of public relations to make the community aware of "expanded informational and educational services."[53]

The following year, when the great demobilization began, librarians relived the experience of their colleagues of the World War I generation. The millions of demobilized struggled with their problems without involving the public library very much. A prominent librarian remarked, "We talk a lot about demobilization and readjustment, library publications are full of it, but are librarians really doing anything about it?" In response, an ALA staffer wrote an article entitled "For the Returning Service Man." The article described the efforts of some sixteen libraries in aiding the demobilized. The Winchester, Massachusetts, Public Library provided a room for use as a veteran's counseling center; Atlanta sent books to a hospital; Akron provided a reading list entitled "They Will Be Coming Back Soon"; Fort Worth provided talking books for blind veterans; Hagerstown, Maryland, provided "a demonstration of library service to returned veterans."[54] The response to the great challenge of demobilization did not amount to much. Librarians again grossly overestimated the extent to which demobilization created needs that could be met by library service.

By the end of the war in August 1945, the attention of the public library community was no longer fixed on demobilization but on defining the role the public library would have in the postwar world.

In October 1945, the ALA Executive Board met to discuss the subject "What is ALA's New Emphasis to Be?" In December, the ALA Council dealt with the question "Where Do We Go Now? What Library Policies and Programs Does the New World Need?"[55] Both discussions were exploratory and inconclusive. Six months later a more definite program was ready. In June 1946, the first seven chapters of the Post-War Planning Committee's *National Plan for Public Library Service* were completed and distributed.

The first chapter of the plan, entitled "The Potential Role of the American Public Library," was written by Lowell Martin. He identified the library as part of the American educational system. In stating the objectives of the public library, he made no reference to those given in the national plans of 1934 and 1939 and in the 1943 standards. According to Martin,

the objectives of the public library are many and various. But in essence they are two—to promote enlightened citizenship and to enrich personal life. They have to do with the twin pillars of the American way, the democratic process of group life, and the sanctity and dignity of the individual person.

Although Martin's essay envisioned the public library primarily as an agency for adult education, that phrase did not appear. In Martin's view, the public library serves its objectives

by the diffusion of information and ideas. By selecting and organizing materials, it makes an educational instrument out of a welter of records. By providing a staff able to interpret materials, it eliminates the gap between the seeker and the sources of enlightenment. When animated by a sense of purpose, reading skill, and community identification, the public library constitutes an important and unique service agency for the citizen. Lacking these attributes, it is a passive badge of culture tolerated by an indifferent populace.[56]

Martin concluded his essay with a passage reminiscent of the Boston trustees' report of 1852: "The public library is potentially an essential unit in the American educational system. . . . It comes closer than any other institution to being the capstone of our educational system."[57]

Succeeding chapters of the plan were written by the planning committee chairman, Carleton B. Joeckel, a library school professor, and Amy Winslow of Baltimore's Enoch Pratt Free Library. Chapter two, entitled "Taking Stock of the American Public Library," was an evaluation of public library service that was originally supposed to be a separate project for the planning committee. Public library service, the chapter concluded, was a mixture of "the best library service in the world and almost the worst." About 37 percent of Americans had good to "potentially good" service; another 37 percent had poor service; the remaining 26 percent had no service at all. Relatively few libraries were adequately funded; buildings and personnel were seriously deficient; libraries were too little used.[58]

Chapters three through seven proposed solutions to the library's problems. Three proposed larger units of service: county libraries, regional libraries, and "federated groups of cooperating libraries."[59] Such libraries could be more adequately funded and staffed than tiny local libraries and would reach previously unserved populations. Chapter four proposed that the states create strong state library agencies to promote the extension of libraries and to supplement service. Chapter four also proposed that state grants-in-aid be awarded to insure minimum levels of support. Chapter five proposed a role for the federal government including a substantial grant program. Chapter six proposed cooperation between public libraries and other types of libraries and among public libraries as well. Chapter seven, entitled "Public Library Finance," presented the financial program for the national plan. At least $200 million annually was needed to support library service to the nation. Of that amount, 60 percent should be obtained locally, 25 percent should be provided by the state, and 15 percent by the federal government. In addition, $500 million was currently needed for building programs, and $175 million for books for new or substandard libraries. The authors acknowledged that "the sums named are large"; but "the American people have, for the most part, been willing from the beginning to tax themselves generously for public education. With public libraries oriented primarily toward educational objectives, funds . . . should be forthcoming."[60]

Chapters eight through thirteen of the plan were finished by July 1947 and were published in January 1948. Chapter eight, entitled "Books and Library Materials," had two key points: library collections should include nonbook materials; and libraries should improve their collections. The most difficult problem was to determine how to "draw the line between the objectives of education and recreation" although "in the post-war years most libraries will doubtless place major emphasis on education. More and more, purely diversional reading will be de-emphasized and left to the commercial agencies. This decision must be made if the library is to perform an educational function worthy of the name."[61]

Shortly before the first seven chapters were distributed, efforts to help implement the plan were under way. On March 12, 1946, a Public Library

Service Demonstration Bill was introduced in Washington, where ALA had opened an office in October of 1945. The bill provided for federal grants of at least $25,000 to each state to be used for demonstrating public library services, primarily in rural areas, "through the use of bookmobiles and library deposits." Demonstrations were regarded as a first step toward establishing regular service. Representative Emily Taft Douglas, who introduced the bill, urged that "we cannot afford to deny large numbers of our people the chance for this basic means of education."[62]

Progress of the bill was slow. When the *National Plan* was finished in 1948, action on the bill was still pending. At that time, the ALA Federal Relations Committee said that passage of the bill would be "a major step in achieving the *National Plan*."[63] The House did not vote on the bill until March 9, 1950; it was defeated by three votes. In 1948, however, there was still hope that the bill would pass and that the *National Plan* would "change the course of the Public Library Movement in North America."[64]

Other matters were also pending in 1948. A big and important project was in progress that was supposed to contribute to postwar public library development, a research project known as the Public Library Inquiry. The inquiry was proposed during the summer of 1946, begun March 1, 1947, and was to take two years to complete. It was being conducted by the Social Science Research Council at ALA's request and was financed by a $200,000 grant from the Carnegie Corporation. The inquiry's purpose as stated by its planning committee, was to provide

a reliable picture of the evolution and trends of library objectives, structure and practice, of present actual library functioning, of unfilled needs, and of alternative possibilities and objectives. Such a picture is intended to serve as a useful basis upon which librarians, library boards and other public officials . . . and citizens concerned with the function of general enlightenment, can frame policy and specific recommendations for the postwar decade or longer.[65]

The authors of the *National Plan* were among those who looked forward to the completion of the inquiry. It would, said the Post-War Planning Committee, "serve to confirm or modify the recommendations of the national plan."[66]

Thus 1947 and 1948 were, in part, years of expectation, of waiting for Congress to provide means for implementing the *National Plan*, and of waiting for the conclusion of the Public Library Inquiry. The plan and the completed inquiry would, it seemed very likely, "make possible a new appraisal of the public library and a new awareness among librarians of their opportunities and responsibilities."[67]

While waiting, however, librarians were not idle. A new and promising development in adult education had appeared on the scene in Chicago and was spreading around the country—the Great Books Program. Small groups whose members had read classic works in literature, philosophy, politics, and other fields met for discussions under the guidance of trained leaders. By 1947, there were sixty-eight groups meeting in programs sponsored by the Chicago Public Library. Library staff members were coleaders of forty of the groups and otherwise involved in the other twenty-eight. Carl Roden, Chicago's librarian, said that the "group technique" used in the programs promised to be "the solution of the baffling problem of library adult education around which all of us have been skittering for the twenty-five years between two world wars."[68] Fern Long, the Cleveland Public Library's Director of Adult Education, viewed the Great Books Program as a "popular educational movement" promising to "sweep the country." A November 1947 *Library Journal* editorial expressed the opinion that "at present, real adult education means education through discussion groups."[69] By 1948, there were Great Books Programs in seventeen cities.[70]

Another large-scale adult education project was launched in 1948. In response to the growing problems of the early postwar years, the ALA Council adopted "a program of action termed the Four Year Goals." The program was created to address "critical problems" which "are international, national, and local; political, economic, and social; racial, agricultural, industrial, ideological, and spiritual. They are not new in themselves. But they are newly dangerous, because they exist in an atomic age." The Four Year Goals were "to be attained in whole or large measure by 1951, the seventy-fifth anniversary of ALA. The goals adopted were:

1. Programs and types of service in every library which will contribute to the awareness and understanding of the urgent problems. 2. Informational and educational materials in every library adequate in quantity, suitable in quality and variety. . . . 3. Good library service for every American. 4. Every library staffed by an adequate number of librarians, competent to perform the public service suggested above.[71]

In order to help promote the attainment of the Four Year Goals, ALA organized the Great Issues Program, a nationwide adult education program dealing with the current problems. The Great Issues were selected by means of a poll of leading authorities carried out by the ALA public relations office. The issues finally selected were: How Much World Government?, Inflation-Deflation, Labor-Management Relations, Civil Rights, and U.S.–Russian Relations. Libraries were asked to provide lectures, study and discussion programs, films, and reading lists. Librarians were urged to inform community groups such as the YMCA, business and veterans organizations, and others concerning their library's program. Librarians were to "push for a community-wide committee" to "coordinate the efforts of all groups," to carry the program to schools and colleges, and to ensure that "the entire library staff" understood the arguments for and against all the issues. E. W. McDiarmid, ALA's president, said that successful promotion of the program would be a "long step . . . toward realization of the Four Year Goals and toward a better informed America."[72] The program began October 1, 1948, with the issue How Much World Government? and ended March 1, 1949, with U.S.–Russian Relations.

The Great Issues Program was a disappointment. In January 1949, an effort was made to evaluate the program by surveying the extent of library participation in the portion of the program scheduled for November 1948 on the subject Inflation-Deflation. Questionnaires were sent to 1,067 libraries. Of the 379 replies, 367 were usable. They revealed that fifty-one libraries participated to some extent in the program, a participation rate a little under 14 percent. Less than 1 percent of the libraries presented the full program of lectures, films, and so on. The author of the survey report concluded that "the picture of the library which emerges from the responses is a disheartening one."[73]

It is difficult to discover what happened to the Four Year Goals program. It disappeared from the index to the *ALA Bulletin* after 1948.

By the end of 1948, the public library had been involved in the adult education movement for a quarter century. For its contribution, it received faint praise. In 1938, Alvin Johnson claimed that no library had developed possibilities for adult education within easy reach. In 1942, John Chancellor, the adult education specialist, said that "so far the contribution of libraries to . . . a more enlightened life for the individual and for society as a whole is very, very slight."[74] In 1945, two members of a subcommittee of ALA's Adult Education Board gave the following assessment:

Library adult education . . . has varied from the specialized services of a readers' adviser to the vague generalization that all library service to adults is adult education. Despite the fact that many libraries have developed effective services to adults, the level of performance lags far behind the objectives set by such recognized authorities as Alvin S. Johnson and William S. Learned. Have not our achievements to date been largely in the field of good public relations rather than genuine education?[75]

And in the *National Plan for Public Library Service*, Lowell Martin observed that "the first hard truth that confronts an observer of American public libraries is that they have stopped far short of their potential. The second truth is that at isolated places, and in partial fashion, they have performed an educational function that is unique and significant."[76] At the end of 1948, it seemed that the Great Issues and Four Year Goals programs were unlikely to provide grounds for evaluations more laudatory than those just quoted.

The library received low marks from the critics because there was no indication of significant progress in the execution of its assigned task, educating the masses. Relatively few people used the library; and of these, only a tiny fraction used it as the documents of the professional community affirmed that it should be used. That is, very few people used the library "to educate themselves continuously." As a people's university, the public library's record was unimpressive at best.

There were offically stated reasons for the library's poor showing. They were presented or implied in plans for library improvement and in appeals for state and federal aid. These reasons were: there were too few libraries; libraries had too little money; advertising and publicity were grossly inadequate; and librarians were too few, poorly qualified, and poorly paid.

Another reason for the unsatisfactory performance of the library was apparently offered informally but rarely published: The public library had contributed little to the enlightenment of the masses because the masses were simply not interested. That relatively few people had the desire to educate themselves was demonstrated by the fact that only a small minority used even the best of libraries; and of this minority, only a small fraction sought enlightenment.

In the 1940s, the public library community was unwilling to consider such an explanation. John Chancellor represented the official position of the community when he said: "It is dodging the issue to say that people do not want . . . educational services. They cannot want what they do not know about and they cannot know and seriously value education until it is redirected toward genuinely useful ends and they begin to see its real accomplishments in the lives of their fellows." By "genuinely useful ends," Chancellor meant helping "the *masses* to learn more about themselves as individual human animals, about their material environments and how to put them under rational control, and about rectifying their relations to others."[77] In 1947, Hiller Wellman, former president of ALA, was corrected when he seemed to suggest that the reason for the library's poor record might somehow lie with the people themselves: "Many of the people, I suspect, were never properly taught to read. . . . Many, ranging from servant girls to highly placed executives, from persons with a limited elementary education to college graduates, for some unknown reason, never read a book. Can these sows' ears be made into silk purses?" Blaming libraries, Wellman said, might be "barking up the wrong tree." Wellman was answered by Olga Peterson, ALA's chief of public relations. Speaking of people who claimed they were too busy to read or didn't like to read, Peterson said: "We know that people are not too busy to do what they really consider important. We suspect that they do not dislike an activity which they find rewarding. It should be within the library's sphere to convince nonreaders that reading is both important and rewarding."[78]

Some observers suggested that the reason for the library's weak performance might be widespread lack of professional dedication to the educational task. In 1938, Alvin Johnson said that the dominant form of professional practice was "pure librarianship," a mode of practice that puts a higher value on circulation than on education. In 1944, the report of the ALA Adult

Education Board stated that "few libraries" are "motivated by an adult education ideal."[79] In 1945, Amy Winslow, a member of the Post-War Planning Committee, said that she did not know "of a single library that has been bold enough to say that education is its main job, this is the way it is going to spend its money, this is the way it is going to put forth its efforts."[80]

But whatever the reasons for the disappointing results of twenty-five years of work in adult education, there seemed to be some cause for optimism at the end of 1948. There was a new *National Plan*. The Library Demonstration Bill was still alive in Washington. And the findings of the Public Library Inquiry would soon be known.

NOTES

1. "Report of the Committee on an Enlarged Program for American Library Service," *ALA Bulletin* 14 (July 1920): 300.

2. Carl H. Milam, "Adult Self-Education," *Public Libraries* 25 (April 1920): 183.

3. Carl B. Roden, "On a Certain Reticence or Inarticulateness among Librarians," *Public Libraries* 28 (November 1923): 489–93.

4. Editorial, *Public Libraries* 28 (November 1923): 501.

5. William S. Learned, *The American Public Library and the Diffusion of Knowledge* (New York: Harcourt Brace, 1924), 6–7.

6. Ibid., 12.

7. Ibid., 56.

8. Judson T. Jennings, "Sticking to Our Last," *ALA Bulletin* 18 (August 1924): 151, 153, 155.

9. Emma Felsenthal, *Readable Books on Many Subjects* (Chicago: American Library Association, 1929), 1.

10. Margaret E. Monroe, *Library Adult Education: The Biography of an Idea* (New York: Scarecrow Press, 1963), 34–35.

11. John Chancellor, Miriam D. Tompkins, and Hazel I. Medway, *Helping the Reader toward Self-Education* (Chicago: American Library Association, 1938), 11.

12. Ibid., 14.

13. Ibid., 19.

14. Ibid., 19–20.

15. J. C. Dana, "Thoughts on the Library and Adult Education," *Library Journal* 53 (November 15, 1928): 945.

16. "The Library and Adult Education: 1924–1934, Ten Year Report," *ALA Bulletin* 29 (June 1935): 318.

17. Jennie M. Flexner, *Reader's Advisers at Work* (New York: American Association for Adult Education, 1941), 64.

18. Margaret M. Herdman, "The Public Library in Depression," *Library Quarterly* 13 (October 1943): 319.

19. "Library Revenues," *ALA Bulletin* 28 (June 1934): 346.

20. "Standards for Public Libraries," *ALA Bulletin* 27 (November 1933): 513.

21. "A National Plan for Libraries," *ALA Bulletin* 29 (February 1935): 91.

22. Ibid., 92–93.

23. Monroe, *Library Adult Education*, 41–42.

24. Miriam D. Tompkins, "Adult Education and the Library School Curriculum," in Louis R. Wilson, ed. *The Role of the Library in Adult Education* (Chicago: University of Chicago Press, 1937), 292.

25. Alvin Johnson, *The Public Library: A People's University* (New York: American Association for Adult Education, 1938), 61.

26. Ibid.

27. Ibid., 30.

28. Ibid., 44.

29. Ibid., 68.

30. Ibid., 59, 65, 68.

31. Ibid., 72, 59.

32. Ibid., 73.

33. Ibid.

34. Ibid., 74.

35. Ibid., 74–75.

36. Ibid., 76–77.

37. Ibid., 77–78.

38. Ibid., 79.

39. Ibid.

40. John Boynton Kaiser, "Problems of Library Finance," in Carleton B. Joeckel, ed. *Current Issues in Library Administration* (Chicago: University of Chicago Press, 1939), 224.

41. "National Defense and the Library," *ALA Bulletin* 35 (January 1941): 5.

42. John Chancellor, "For a Free and Enlightened People," *ALA Bulletin* 35 (April 1941): 198.

43. Franklin D. Roosevelt, "Proclamation," *ALA Bulletin* 36 (January 1942): 2.

44. "Libraries and the War," *ALA Bulletin* 36 (January 1942): 3.

45. Rose L. Vormelker, "Cleveland's War Informative Center," *Library Journal* 67 (April 15, 1942): 349.

46. Elmer Davis, "A Message to American Librarians," *ALA Bulletin* 36 (October 1, 1942): 583.

47. Marion Metcalf Root, "Cataloging and Classification in Wartime," *ALA Bulletin* 36 (December 1, 1942): 831.

48. John Chancellor, "The Diffusion of Knowledge: A Memorandum," *ALA Bulletin* 36 (September 1, 1942): 556.

49. ALA Committee on Post-War Planning, *Post-War Standards for Public Libraries* (Chicago: American Library Association, 1943), 9.

50. Ibid., 22–23.

51. Carleton B. Joeckel, "Library Planning: A General View," *ALA Bulletin* 38 (February 1944): 35–36.

52. Floyd W. Rieves and Carl Vitz, "Demobilization and Readjustment and the Library," *ALA Bulletin* 38 (February 1944): 48–49.

53. "Demobilization and the Library: A Manifesto," *ALA Bulletin* 38 (April 1944): 130–31.

54. Margaret Fulmer, "For the Returning Service Man," *ALA Bulletin* 39 (June 1945): 197–98.

55. "What Is ALA's New Emphasis to Be?" *ALA Bulletin* 39 (December 1, 1945):

481–87. "Where Do We Go Now? What Library Policies and Programs Does the New World Need?" *ALA Bulletin* 40 (March 1946): 83–88.

56. ALA Committee on Post-War Planning, *A National Plan for Public Library Service* (Chicago: American Library Association, 1948), 16.

57. Ibid., 16–17.

58. Ibid., 31–32.

59. Ibid., 53.

60. Ibid., 95–96.

61. Ibid., 107–08.

62. "Library Demonstration Bill Introduced," *ALA Bulletin* 40 (April 1946): 122.

63. ALA Federal Relations Committee, "Report," *ALA Bulletin* 42 (October 15, 1948): 417.

64 ALA Committee on Post-War Planning, *A National Plan for Public Library Service*, v.

65. "The Public Library Inquiry," *Library Journal* 72 (May 1, 1947): 720.

66. ALA Committee on Post-War Planning, "Report," *ALA Bulletin* 41 (October 15, 1947): 352.

67. John S. Richards, "The National Plan for Public Library Service," *ALA Bulletin* 41 (September 1, 1947): 283.

68. "The Great Books Program," *ALA Bulletin* 40 (April 1946): 119.

69. Monroe, *Library Adult Education*, 54.

70. Lynn E. Birge, *Serving Adult Learners: A Public Library Tradition* (Chicago: American Library Association, 1981), 76.

71. "Four Year Goals," *ALA Bulletin* 42 (March 1948): 121–22.

72. "The Great Issues," *Booklist* 44 (August 1948): 397–99.

73. Lester Asheim, "Response to the Great Issues Program," *ALA Bulletin* 44 (July-August 1950): 285–89.

74. John Chancellor, "The Diffusion of Knowledge," 556.

75. "Preparation for Library Adult Education," *ALA Bulletin* 39 (April 1945): 259.

76. ALA Committee on Post-War Planning, *A National Plan for Public Library Service*, 3.

77. John Chancellor, "The Diffusion of Knowledge," 556.

78. "Should All People Read?" *ALA Bulletin* 41 (October 1947): 320–21.

79. ALA Adult Education Board, "The Educational Role of Libraries," *ALA Bulletin* 38 (October 1, 1944): 341.

80. "What Is ALA's New Emphasis to Be?" 486.

5

The Public Library Inquiry

1948–1950

The reports of the Public Library Inquiry began to appear in the summer of 1949. Librarians had been anticipating the reports for more than two years.

But the reports were part of a much longer sequence of events. Ever since 1934, leaders of the public library community had been planning to make the public library a stronger educational institution, to create more effective institutional forms, to extend library service, and to secure more adequate and stable financial support. Since the beginning of World War II, the planning enterprise had become more serious and intense. The war, the emergence of the United States as the world's principal military and economic power, the development of atomic energy, the postwar menace of communism, the burgeoning problems of industrial relations and civil rights—all seemed to require an immense effort of popular education. The American people, it seemed, were called upon to attain levels of intellectual and political sophistication previously unnecessary in a less complex and less dangerous world.

The leading intellectuals of the public library community had been planning and working ever since 1942, at least, to make the public library the instrument that would provide the needed sophistication, the needed enlightenment. The standards of 1943, the *National Plan* of 1948, and the effort since 1946 to secure passage of federal legislation were all part of the plan, part of the work. Finally, the Public Library Inquiry was to provide the knowledge indispensable to the whole enterprise. The most extensive and competent study of the public library ever conducted was to enable the public library community to put all the pieces together so that the public library could become the important and effective educational institution it was capable of becoming. The long-awaited findings of the inquiry would reveal with unprecedented clarity and authority what public-spirited and consci-entious librarians should do to make the public library the instrument of popular education that they devoutly and fervently believed it could be.

But as it turned out, the inquiry offered no such revelation. On the contrary, the principal findings of the inquiry indicated that the public library could never be an instrument of popular education; and the principal recommendation of the inquiry counseled the public library community to abandon the attempt to make it such an instrument.

The findings and recommendations of the inquiry had a profound and lasting impact on the public library community. It destroyed the traditional faith and confidence of leading intellectuals in the library community; it shocked and demoralized the public library community as a whole. The inquiry made it impossible for librarians to contemplate and to talk about the public library in the old way with the old conviction, and offered nothing satisfactory by way of replacement. The public library community was cast adrift from the old moorings and has been trying to deal with the consequences ever since. This chapter is the story of the inquiry. The chapters that follow are, to a great extent, the story of the public library community struggling with the consequences of the inquiry.

The inquiry reports consisted of seven books published by the Columbia University Press and five special reports put out by various publishers. The two most important books were: *The Library's Public* by Bernard Berelson, dean of the library school at the University of Chicago, and *The Public Library in the United States: The General Report of the Public Library Inquiry* by Robert D. Leigh, a political scientist who was director of the inquiry. The impact of the inquiry on the public library community was determined primarily by these two books.

Berelson's book—an extensive investigation of library users and use and of the impact of mass media—presented his major findings and conclusions. About 25 to 30 percent of American adults read at least one book a month. About half the adult population saw at least one motion picture every two weeks. About 90 percent read a newspaper regularly and listened to the radio daily. Book reading was thus relatively limited.

Of the books read by American adults, the public library supplied about one-fourth. About 18 percent of adults used the public library once a year. About 10 percent used the library once a month. That 10 percent together with the 33 percent of children and young people who used the library once a month "might be considered the real users of the public library."[1] Also, there was "a heavy concentration of library use by a small group of frequent borrowers."[2] Five percent of library users borrowed about 40 percent of the books circulated annually. Twenty percent of users borrowed 70 percent of the books. Of the books borrowed, nearly half were juvenile; about two-thirds were fiction. Nonfiction borrowing was concentrated among a small group of students and well-educated adults.[3]

Concerning other library materials and services, Berelson reported that the public was barely aware of the library as a source of information. Reference service was heavily used by students for school assignments. Most adults who used that service did so for "fact-finding"; up to 90 percent of reference questions asked by adults "call for brief, simple answers."[4] Newspapers and magazines in public libraries were used mostly for reference. Professional services other than reference were relatively inconsequential. Librarians had "little effect upon the reading tastes and interests of the adult public."[5]

Major findings concerning library users indicated that the young used the library more than older people; women used it more than men; and the well educated used it more than the less educated. "The public library serves the middle class, defined either by occupation or by economic status."[6] Users who expressed dissatisfaction complained mostly about inadequate book collections; relatively few found fault with librarians.

The general public regarded the library as a "fine thing for a community to have"[7] even though the public had little knowledge of the library and its services. A survey of the general public conducted in several large cities by the National Opinion Research Center revealed that only 2 percent of those surveyed said it would make little difference to the city if there were no public library. Seventy-eight percent said it would make a "great deal" of difference; 16 percent said "quite a bit." At the same time, however, 61 percent said it would make "not much" difference to them personally if there were no public library.[8]

In the final chapter, Berelson presented the implications of the previous chapters:

It may well be that the proper role of the public library is deliberately and consciously to serve the "serious" and "culturally alert" members of the community rather than attempt now to reach all the people.... The research literature ... clearly demonstrates that universality of public library service is practically impossible at the present time, regardless of the aggressiveness of the public library in promoting itself. It may be, therefore, that the librarian should explicitly redefine his goal from attempting to serve the total community to providing the minority of "serious" users ... with the tools which they need.... The library's attempt to serve the total community is bound to bring disappointment and perhaps deterioration in the quality of its service. The library serves a small clientele today; it would lose no prestige by serving an even smaller group with a higher quality of service.[9]

Berelson went on to state further implications. The library could not contribute much to the political enlightenment of the masses. The people most in need of such enlightenment did not use the library and "probably cannot be attracted to the public library for this purpose.... Other channels of communication" must perform the task of public enlightenment. Another implication is that the public library "might leave the field of popular entertainment to the commercial media."[10]

Robert D. Leigh's book, *The Public Library in the United States*, incorporated the works of Berelson and other inquiry researchers. It was the general report of the inquiry and contained the inquiry's general recommendations.

After briefly describing the inquiry and some of its basic assumptions, Leigh presented the "objectives" of the public library. His statement of objectives was formulated by combining the major statements of public library purpose issued during recent years: the statement from the 1943 standards which was based on the National Plans of the 1930s, the statement from the 1948 National Plan, and the one from the Four Year Goals of 1948. Leigh's statement included key phrases from the earlier documents. The objectives of the library were to promote "enlightened citizenship and enriched personal lives, to serve the community as a . . . center of reliable information, to provide opportunity and encouragement" for people "to educate themselves continously. . . . to improve people's ability to participate usefully in activities in which they are involved as citizens," to help people "improve their capacity for appreciation and production in cultural fields. . . . to help people make such use of leisure time as will promote personal happiness and social well-being," to help people aid "in the advancement of knowledge," and so on. No important phrase from the earlier documents was left out.[11] Following the statement of objectives was a list of "means" for attaining the objectives. The list concluded with the statement that between 1948 and 1952 libraries should change "the nature of their services" in order to "contribute directly to the solution of the crucial problems of our time." Libraries should ensure that "citizens have the widest possible range of reliable information" even if this meant "some curtailment of acquisition of popular and general materials."[12]

Leigh's statement of objectives had been tested by surveying librarians throughout the country. Sixty public libraries of all sizes constituted the inquiry's research sample. The statement was also sent to eleven additional librarians in large cities, nineteen state librarians, eleven library school professors, and ten other persons who were university librarians or "library officials" interested in the public library. Of the eighty-eight who responded, 84 percent "accepted the statement of objectives as sound and accurate."[13]

The remaining 16 percent found the statement of objectives unsatisfactory. The major objection was that the statement included no provision for meeting public demand. This, the dissenters claimed, made the statement of objectives "wrong and impractical." The library should provide books, "good or bad, for all comers." Leigh conceded that the objectives did not provide for "entertainment" or "amusement"; they were not part of what the statement meant by recreation. The minority of dissenters, Leigh claimed, "renounce the librarian's faith in the ameliorative function of books" which was affirmed by the vast majority of those surveyed.[14]

Concluding this chapter, Leigh considered the possibility that the objectives approved by the majority might be like a party platform, affirmed out of expediency but ignored in practice. The test of objectives was whether they actually guided day-to-day practice and had a "vital relationship to social needs." Before accepting the objectives as a "fixed framework" for examining the public library, it was necessary to establish their "appropriateness."[15] This could be done by considering the relationship of the public library to other agencies of public communication, which was the subject of Leigh's third chapter, "The Business of Communication."

Leigh began with a discussion of mass media and their audiences. He summarized Berelson's findings on book reading and library use and users. Leigh then described some characteristics of the commercial mass media. They concentrated on celebrities, were prone to sensationalism and distortion, avoided the unpopular, and focused on "events and interests of the moment."[16] Because of these characteristics, the commercial mass media were ill suited to the performance of certain important tasks of public communication. Finally, Leigh indicated the point of his analysis of the mass media: it enabled one to "discern the natural and appropriate role of the public library in our society."[17] This role was not to compete with the mass media, but to provide services of the kind they could not provide. The natural role of the public library was "to serve the group of adults whose interest, will and ability lead them to seek personal enrichment and enlightenment." This group constituted the "natural public library audience." Although this audience was a minority, it included many persons important to the community. Service to this group was socially important.[18]

Leigh then described the services that were appropriate for this natural audience. The library should serve as a center for the most authoritative and reliable materials produced each year; as a center for materials providing full and balanced views of unpopular or new ideas; as a center for materials of enduring high quality; and as a center where the complete record, in print and on recordings and films, could be focused on particular subjects or problems. These services were not likely to be performed by the commercial mass media. Furthermore, Leigh concluded, these services were fully consistent with the statement of objectives presented in chapter two. Those objectives "seem to mark the almost inevitable road for public libraries to follow if they are to play their appropriate role as a public agency of communication."[19]

In succeeding chapters, Leigh summarized the findings and conclusions of other phases of the inquiry. In the concluding chapter, he endorsed the recommendations of the 1948 *National Plan* calling for larger units of service and state and federal aid. Such units and financial aid would be helpful in enabling the library to assume its distinctive communication role, serve its natural audience, and attain the objectives set forth at the beginning of the report.

The initial reaction of the professional community to the Public Library Inquiry was a strong one. Predictably, the reaction focused on Berelson's

book, Leigh's analysis of the business of communication, and Leigh's conclusion about the library's natural audience, natural role, and appropriate
services.

The reaction came quickly. In anticipation of the inquiry's completion, a
conference on the inquiry had been planned for August 8–13, 1949, by the
library school at the University of Chicago. Interest was high. The conference
on the inquiry drew the largest audience ever to attend one of these annual
meetings.

Berelson's book was the subject of a paper delivered by Lowell Martin,
then associate dean of the library school at Columbia University. In his
opening remarks, Martin observed that others before Berelson had reported
that public libraries were used mostly by a minority of younger, well-educated persons. But the earlier reports failed to compel the attention of librarians. Berelson, however, presented the facts "in impressive array"; and
librarians could not "dodge this blast."[20] Martin did not contest the facts;
but he wished that Berelson had revealed the reasons why library use was
so limited.

Martin's main concern was discovering a course of action for librarians to
take since they now had to face the facts of life. He considered the advisability
of following Berelson's recommendation that the library concentrate its efforts
on the small minority of serious users. Martin wondered about this. The
public library, he said, had already "reached" this group. Would the library's
impact be strengthened by concentrating efforts on it? Next, Martin considered what might be done to increase the number of library users. Two
possibilities were lowering book-selection standards and buying more du-
plicates of popular books. But the problem here was answering the question,
"to what end or purpose?" Another possibility was accepting the present
minority of library users as the library's proper public and trying to improve
service. "Pragmatic grounds," Martin said, favored this possibility. This
public was at least established. Hypothetical other publics might or might
not be out there. Finally, librarians might offer entirely new programs. But
no one had said what these might be. Thus, according to Martin, there were
several possibilities. He had questions about all but the "pragmatic" one.[21]

In the last section of his discussion, Martin tried to formulate a specific
recommendation. First, he considered the prospects for the library as an
educational institution. There were hardly grounds for being "starry-eyed"
about those prospects. Book reading was of little interest to the majority of
Americans; most books read were ephemeral. There was little support for
adult education.[22] Having said this, Martin interrupted his discussion of
educational prospects and described another possible "function" for the library—the "supply function," which meant finding out what people wanted
and supplying it "as economically and satisfactorily" as possible. Bookstores
and rental libraries were competitors; but "with ingenuity," the library might
well keep its "place as a supplier."[23] Martin then returned to the library's

educational prospects. He offered the "foremost" reason why the library was not succeeding as an educational institution. It was not what his earlier comments led one to expect, namely, the low estate of book reading and adult education in America. The "foremost" problem is the failure of librarians to define their "goals."[24] Here Martin struck a false note. The public library's educational goals were set forth as clearly as they could be in official statements of library objectives. Martin wrote one of the most important himself; and the statement at the beginning of Leigh's inquiry report was both clear and full. Martin offered no example to indicate the nature of a clearly defined goal. He said only that until such a definition was forthcoming, "the library would be wise to let its supply function predominate." It would not be wise to neglect established services and clienteles and resort to "ill-conceived" innovations that might lack public support. The library might vanish "in the fog of its own idealism."[25]

This warning was followed by a weak and confused recommendation that the library maintain its "educational aspirations"; but Martin's position was clear. Educational programs offered by the public library were unlikely to attract public support. Martin did not wish to conclude his discussion by asserting that this was because Americans were simply not interested, so he blamed librarians. They had not been able to clarify their educational goals. Until they did, business as usual was the safe course.

Berelson's response to the discussion of his book was brief. He reported his "surprise and dismay" at the negative reaction his book had provoked.[26] Librarians seemed to hold him personally responsible for the facts he reported. He denied that the reasons for such limited library use were as unclear as Martin suggested, observing that the reasons why educated people predominated among library users were apparent. They were able to read well. Education had stimulated their interest in reading.

Berelson then went on to observe that public librarians had two sets of objectives. One set of "actual" objectives was generally unstated, had evolved out of library history, and was reflected in library practice. These objectives were primarily responsible for the facts concerning the library's public. The other set, consisting of objectives formulated by "official bodies," identified professional aspirations. When objectives were publicly stated, they were the official objectives. Thus, says Berelson, librarians proclaimed educational objectives while they worked to "increase circulation."[27]

Leigh's report was discussed by Ralph W. Tyler, a social scientist and member of the University of Chicago faculty. Tyler took issue with the survey method Leigh used to establish library objectives, but praised the report as the kind of work that would help to improve the library as librarians become more conscious of its important educational role.

Following discussions of the other inquiry reports, a summary of the conference was presented by Ralph Munn, director of the Carnegie Library of Pittsburgh. Librarians should accept the fact, Munn said, that a large majority of Americans do not read books at all; and very few Americans indeed read serious books. Also, librarians should agree that the mass media offer sufficient opportunities for entertainment and escape. Librarians should recognize that they can make the greatest contribution to American society by limiting library activities to those that are consistent with the claim that the library is an "educational and cultural institution."[28] Munn claimed that this course need not reduce the number of library users. New, specialized services to business, labor, and other groups, combined with more effective publicity, would enable the library to attract more users.

Munn said that the changes necessary to implement inquiry recommendations could be made in "larger cities" without provoking serious public resistance. There should, however, be "no public announcements of a purely restrictive nature." Also, library staffs must be convinced that the changes were necessary; and this might be difficult.[29]

Concluding his summary, Munn acknowledged that there were times when it seemed to him that the inquiry was "the obituary of the public library." But, he decided, the library was still alive. Only "the mass of folklore" with which librarians have "surrounded the library" had passed away: "The library does not and cannot have universal appeal. The peoples do not thirst for knowledge. The world is not waiting for a book. . . . These myths are dead. The Inquiry . . . has cut away all the fantastically exaggerated ideas with which we have sought to bolster our faith." But, said Munn, the inquiry had provided something better than myths: it had provided facts. It had clarified the status of the library in relation to the mass media, identified potential users, and set forth "aims and objectives which are attainable." Munn hoped that he and other librarians would use the facts "boldly in revising our course."[30]

The conference in Chicago seemed to encourage the view that the inquiry would inaugurate a new era for the public library. According to Leigh, no one at the Chicago conference challenged Berelson's recommendation that the library's proper role was to serve the serious user. Leigh apparently did not view Martin's comments as dissent. It was soon clear, however, that challenges would not be lacking.

In 1949, ALA did not hold a national conference. Instead, there were seven regional conferences held during September, October, and November. Librarians met in Florida, Massachusetts, New Jersey, Texas, Michigan, Colorado, and British Columbia. A discussion of the inquiry was part of the program at all seven. Leigh was present at all of the conferences and wrote a brief report describing them. At the conferences, reactions to Berelson's book were "extremely negative." His findings and the implications he drew from them were characterized as "extremely depressing," "a kick in the teeth," undemocratic, and defeatist. The criticism of Berelson, Leigh says, was "emotional rather than closely reasoned." The statement of objectives in Leigh's book was also one of the principal subjects of discussion at the conferences. The discussions, said Leigh, made it clear that the objectives were not consistent with the purchase and circulation of "ephemeral current fiction." Some librarians—Leigh did not indicate how many—"rejected the plainly educational function" that the objectives assign to the library. The function of the library according to those librarians was to provide what people want "irrespective of quality, reliability or value."[31]

Brief reports on the regional conferences were published in the *ALA Bulletin*; but they were not very informative. The authors of the reports were strangely reticent. The report on the Massachusetts conference (1,136 registrants) said that "capacity audiences were stimulated" by the discussion.[32] The report on the New Jersey conference (more than 1,000 registrants) said that Ralph Munn told the audience the inquiry reports were "devastating to read because they exposed the mass of folklore with which we surround the library." He recommended that the library concentrate on serving "opinion leaders" in the community. No audience reaction was reported.[33] The report of the Michigan conference (1,196 registrants) merely said that the inquiry was discussed and that one discussion was "spirited."[34] The report of the Colorado conference (over 500 registrants) said that the discussion of the inquiry was the "highlight of the conference" and that librarians realized from the discussion that the inquiry reports "will be required reading."[35] The report of the British Columbia conference (753 librarians attended) made no mention of the inquiry discussion but referred to a comment published elsewhere that librarians at the British Columbia conference showed considerable interest in the inquiry.[36] No reports of the Florida and Texas conferences were published.

A brief note in *Public Libraries* was more informative than the five reports published in the *ALA Bulletin*. *Public Libraries* reported that many who attended the seven regional conferences did not have access to the inquiry publications "so anything like general discussion was impossible." There was some discussion, however, and "the most spirited . . . seems to have centered around the question of the library concentrating on an elite or intellectually alert group; whether public libraries should withdraw from the recreational field, and the place of children's work in the public library." The inquiry reports, the note concluded, "will be read and discussed for years to come."[37]

At the ALA midwinter meeting in Chicago during late January 1950, the inquiry was the subject of a symposium sponsored by the Division of Public Libraries, the Trustee's Division, and the Extension Division. The title of the symposium, "If Not the People's University, Then What?" referred to a relatively minor point in Leigh's book, his recommendation that public libraries serve adult education agencies as the library of the people's university. The symposium was introduced as "one of the first reappraisals of the place of the public library in the light of the Public Library Inquiry. Each public librarian who stops to ask himself, 'Quo Vadis'—will find help here in formulating an answer."[38]

Four papers were read, the first by an adult education specialist from the University of Louisville. The paper gave a brief status report on adult education in America and a description of some cooperative adult education programs involving the University of Louisville and the Louisville Public Library.

The second paper was by Emerson Greenaway, director of the Enoch Pratt Free Library in Baltimore. After a discussion of some alternative possibilities for library participation in adult education, Greenaway made five recommendations for the "decade to come":

1. That public libraries accept as their basic objectives the provision and servicing of expertly selected books and other materials which aid the individual in the pursuit of education, information, or research, and in the creative use of leisure time. . . . The library should recognize that its *major* concern must be a positive contribution toward the removal of ignorance, intolerance and indifference.

2. That we recognize educational service to adults as a primary function. . . .

3. That we accept the responsibility for the direct communication of ideas through organization of discussion groups, institutes, film forums and the like. . . .

4. That we frankly state that in meeting its objective of providing recreational materials, the library encourage such use of leisure time as will promote personal development and social well-being, and tend increasingly to leave to commercial agencies the provision of trivial, purely ephemeral materials.[39]

Greenaway's fifth recommendation urged cooperation with other educational agencies.

The third paper was presented by Ralph A. Ulveling, director of the Detroit Public Library. His paper rambled over a collection of four "points" that he feels "must be corrected if we are to move forward toward the realization of our best purposes." These points were that librarians must find a new measure of effectiveness to replace circulation statistics. Librarians should change book selection standards. They should be less concerned about the popularity of books and choose "every book . . . primarily from the standpoint of the positive contribution it can make to individuals." The third point was that libraries need staff with "psychological skills" who see library work "in terms of people." The fourth was that libraries should use films to provide education, not recreation. Ulveling concluded his paper by stating that the library existed to promote the intellectual independence of individuals; and the library was, therefore, the people's university.[40]

The fourth paper was presented by the state librarian of Washington. The focus of her paper was library extension, and she thus did not deal with the assigned topic.

At the ALA conference in July 1950, the Adult Education Section of the Public Libraries Division held a panel discussion with the same title as the midwinter symposium, "If Not the People's University, Then What?" The proceedings of the ALA conference reported only that "the panel discussed the importance of adult education in the world today and the role librarians should play."[41]

The inquiry was the subject of many speeches and discussions at state and local meetings of librarians. By one count, the inquiry was discussed at "70 sessions" around the country during 1949;[42] and the discussions and speeches continued through mid–1950. Speeches given at some of the meeting were printed in the library press. Most reports of the meetings gave no indication of audience reaction to speakers or panels.

In November 1949, Gertrude Gscheidle of the Chicago Public Library addressed a meeting of the Illinois Library Association. She summarized Leigh's report and gave her view of the implications of the inquiry:

The provision of materials old and new, for information, education and reference use by adult citizens is a function performed by no other communications agency. It is consequently in this area that the public library can make its greatest contribution. . . . What is therefore indicated is a "sobering up" with a declining emphasis on entertainment and recreation and a growing emphasis on developing and publicizing the informational, educational and reference services.[43]

No audience reaction was indicated.

In November 1949, John Mackenzie Cory, the executive secretary of ALA, gave an address entitled "The Public Library Inquiry" to a meeting of Arkansas librarians. His speech was essentially a straightforward summary of Leigh's report. There was no indication of how his speech was received.[44]

In January 1950, a meeting of Public Library Executives of Southern California discussed the question, "Is a Public Library Justified in Limiting Its Service?" The discussion focused on Berelson's book, *The Library's Public*, and on a Los Angeles Public Library (*LAPL*) study entitled *Objectives of the Library*. The "target for attack, as it were, was the implication by Berelson and the recommendation of the LAPL survey that public libraries discontinue the provision of light fiction including romances, westerns and mysteries." The target was thoroughly attacked: "No group of librarians present seemed to agree with the recommendation that libraries ban light fiction." The author of a report on the discussion was the librarian of the San Bernardino County Library. In her trips around the county, she said, people asked her, "You don't really mean you're going to stop furnishing mysteries—do you?—or westerns, as the case may be." She concluded her report by saying that she and the San Bernardino board of supervisors "believe that light fiction cannot and should not be eliminated from the San Bernardino County Library at this time."[45]

In March 1950, the inquiry was discussed by a group of 450 attending a meeting of the California Library Association Southern District at Pomona. Harold L. Hammil, librarian of the Los Angeles Public Library, summarized the inquiry. His remarks were followed by a discussion. On the whole, the audience displayed

a somewhat cool reserve in the face of the Inquiry's scientific probing. . . . The general attitude toward the Inquiry was something like the reaction of the people of Delake, Ore., when the body of a strange bedraggled sea beast was recently cast up on their shore by the surf. They were curious about the oddity of the deep, but not many were willing to get very close to it. . . . There was a general feeling of apprehension and discomfort. Most agreed they didn't like the smell of the thing.

During a discussion of Berelson's book, librarians from small libraries expressed a "fear . . . that elimination of ephemeral books would put them out of business." Relatively few present at the discussion of Berelson's book had read it. Indeed, there was "general ignorance of the content of the Inquiry volumes." The author of the report on the Pomona meeting concludes by noting that "representatives of larger libraries generally were disposed to accept the Inquiry as a serious contribution, compelling critical attention."[46]

In April 1950, Edward B. Hayward of the Racine Public Library addressed a meeting of librarians from southern Wisconsin. His speech was entitled "A Positive Approach to *The Library's Public*." After summarizing Berelson's findings, Hayward observed that the average adult "spends about one-fourth of his waking hours being educated, recreated and entertained; but the library's share of this time is small." What should the library do about this? "The suggestion put forward by Mr. Berelson—that we redefine our goal from attempting to serve the total community to the providing of books for the minority of serious users and seekers of information—seems to me neither a politic nor a practical course for the average, existing public library." Hayward did not explain or argue his position; he immediately went on to indicate what he regarded as the proper response to Berelson's findings. Hayward recommended studying the community, analyzing library activities, providing staff "trained to meet the needs of distinctive community groups," providing recordings and films in order to attract new users, making the library more convenient and pleasant for library users, and providing better service through cooperation with other libraries. "New groups can be reached," Hayward concluded. "Once the true facts about a library's public are known, a positive course of action can be determined."[47] There was no indication of audience reaction to Hayward's speech.

In May 1950, Margaret E. Davidson, librarian of the Webster City, Iowa, Public Library, addressed two meetings of the Iowa Library Association. Her speech, entitled "The PLI and You," was presented at both meetings. Davidson strongly recommended the inquiry reports. Her speech, she said was a campaign to push the inquiry volumes "toward best seller lists." Concluding a summary of Berelson's book, she said: "All of this report—especially the pretty well established fact that public libraries at best and no matter how exotic their publicity—reach only a small group of people, has caused a pretty flutter in the dovecote of ALA." Of the inquiry reports as a group, Davidson said, "There is positively not a dull page anywhere. If all of us would read all of the volumes of the Public Library Inquiry, the impetus of our enthusiasm would carry the public library movement forward fifty years in the next decade."[48] There was no indication whether her audiences shared her enthusiasm.

From August 1950 to January 1951, *Library Journal* published a light flurry of correspondence dealing with the inquiry. Most of the items were published as letters; one was published in a regular feature entitled "Good Ideas," another in *Library Journal*'s "Professional Reading" section.

The item in the "Professional Reading" section of the August 1950 issue was by Eli Oboler, a university librarian in Idaho. Oboler remarked that "there has been surprisingly little discussion in print, as yet, of the Public Library Inquiry." He believed this was because the inquiry was still too recent. The rest of Oboler's piece was an attack on Berelson and on the implications drawn from his study. Berelson's position was denounced as defeatist and undemocratic. Oboler offered his own idea of the implications of *The Library's Public*: "Get busy, public librarians. Use all the techniques at your command to 'sell' your service to your community." Oboler closed with the question: "Will the non-elite taxpayers be willing to pay for a public library serving only the elite?"[49]

In the "Good Ideas" feature of the September 15, 1950, issue *Library Journal* published an item from Margaret Paulus, librarian of the West Allis, Wisconsin, Public Library. Paulus objected to the "scorn" with which the inquiry treated "recreational aspects of public library service." Her reaction at first was "doubt and surprise" passing "to a state of very active resistance. Why not recreation?" she asked. The community supported tennis, square dancing, and other forms of recreation; why not reading "just for the fun of it"? Public library fiction was better than drugstore fiction and might lead to a "widening horizon." Fiction reading might keep young people from seeking recreation that was not "advisable." Paulus concludes by saying that "if I find that I must cast three-quarters of my public into outer darkness I think I'll go right along with them."[50] *Library Journal* received four letters applauding Paulus.

The October 1, 1950, issue of *Library Journal* published a letter from John F. Carroll, an employee in the library division of a publisher. Carroll had attended four of the ALA regional conferences of the previous year at which the inquiry was discussed. The discussions led him to the conclusion that the inquiry was a waste of money. The money should have been spent on a public relations campaign to "acquaint the American taxpayer and voter with the wonderful services available in the public library."[51]

The November 15 issue published a letter from a staff member of the New York Public Library, Robert E. Kingery, who wrote of two matters that "disturb" him and "have their origins in various pages of LJ." One was the "easy assumption" that identified the library's recreational role with the reading of light fiction. More important for "re-creating persons" were "books on crafts and hobbies, the creative literature, music, art and all the other books that open up avenues of expression and self-realization." The other matter that disturbed Kingery was "the mounting rejection of the Public Library Inquiry."[52]

By the end of 1950, the inquiry had been thoroughly discussed at meetings; several of the speeches had been published; and a few correspondents had vented their feelings in library periodicals. There seemed to be considerable opposition to the inquiry's principal recommendations; but none of this opposition had appeared as reasoned published argument. There was also support for the inquiry's recommendations, especially among some leading librarians of large cities.[53] But the question remained: What position, amply considered and justified, would the public library community finally take on the inquiry? There had been no significant exchange of views in print. Professional organizations had taken no stand.

The inquiry called for the public library to adopt a new role in American society and marshaled impressive arguments in favor of adopting that role. The public library community seemed to be faced with a choice. It could accept the inquiry's recommendations or reject them. Acceptance could be justified with arguments furnished by the inquiry itself. Rejection called for counterarguments disclosing the flaws in the position taken by the inquiry and indicating why the best interests of American society justified its rejection.

Late in 1950, there still seemed reason to believe that more adequate published discussion of the inquiry would be forthcoming. The ALA Executive Board met in Washington, D.C., in late October. "The Public Library Inquiry was discussed at some length. Steps were approved to publicize the list of reports resulting from the Inquiry and the hope was expressed that all groups within the ALA would study and act on appropriate findings and recommendations in the reports. A number of library staffs and library schools are engaged actively in analysis of the Inquiry."[54] The outcome of such analysis would, presumably, be a discussion in print sifting the inquiry and its recommendations. Such a discussion was necessary if the public library community was to take a position and if ALA or its Public Libraries Division was to take a formal stand on the inquiry.

But the discussion never took place. Library school faculty members may have analyzed the inquiry, but they had nothing to say in print. Analysis by library staffs produced a letter to the editors of the *Wilson Library Bulletin* early in 1951.[55] By the middle of that year, it was fairly apparent that the public library community would take no further notice of the inquiry. There would be no public discussion; professional organizations would take no position. Henceforth, the inquiry would simply be ignored.

There was some protest at the treatment the inquiry received; but it was mild and ineffective. In October 1951, *Library Journal* published some responses to an "informal LJ survey." The journal had asked some readers what kinds of articles they would like to see in the publication. One reader wrote: "I wish that we could have some constructive discussions on the Public Library Inquiry." Another wrote: "I do not think that the library profession or the professional magazines have given this subject nearly the attention it deserves. It seems necessary to me to keep this subject alive for the next year or two until librarians are forced to make decisions about the important suggestions included in the Inquiry."[56] But the matter had been decided; the inquiry was to be ignored.

The informal compact to ignore the inquiry was faithfully observed. The rank and file, the leaders, and the professional organizations all maintained silence. How can this be explained?

Virtually everyone in the public library community had reason to favor or tolerate the silent treatment given the inquiry. The silence of a large majority of librarians can probably be explained without difficulty. This majority consisted partly of those who were silent from simple self-interest, the ones who believed, whether they said so or not, that following inquiry recommendations would put them out of business. That position was hard to justify theoretically. One could hardly speak in favor of a role for the public library because that role secured one's job. Librarians whose opposition to the inquiry was thus based on a reason that could not be stated took comfort in silence.

The other part of the silent majority of librarians consisted of those who, regardless of their appraisal of the inquiry's value, would have been silent anyway because of timidity or lack of talent or disposition for public discussion. They might have wished for a discussion and have observed it with interest; but they would not have spoken.

The silence of leaders of the public library community, those who were accustomed to speaking out, was a little more difficult to understand. A few, perhaps, were silent from sheer embarrassment. The great postwar plans had envisioned the public library as the agency of political enlightenment and intellectual enrichment for the masses. In the light cast by the inquiry, those plans appeared naive and utopian. A discussion of the inquiry was likely to call attention to the extravagance of postwar plans, so some of their designers, at least, had reason to favor or tolerate silence.

Another more subtle pressure worked in favor of silence. Public library theory had always assumed that the masses want and seek the knowledge that is the condition of their political fitness and their development as intellectually adequate human beings. The inquiry strongly suggested that such an assumption was dubious or unwarranted. Americans in general do not relish public discussions that delve into the disposition of the people to pursue enlightenment. Such discussions threaten to raise troubling questions. If ignorance is the preferred and inevitable condition of the vast majority of the people, then American democratic theory may be seriously defective. A public discussion of the inquiry might easily venture into dangerous territory. It would not be surprising if librarians had no inclination to get involved in one. Librarians who believed, as the inquiry suggested, that the masses are content to be ignorant had no wish to say so. Librarians who believed otherwise had the imposing weight of the inquiry in the balance against them. Avoiding serious public discussion of the inquiry promised to be the most comfortable course of action for both groups.

In addition, circumstances conspired to promote silence. The climate of 1951 made silence agreeable and expedient and made insistence on discussing the inquiry seem disloyal or perverse.

Right after the Library Demonstration Bill failed in March 1950, work began on new legislation. A Library Service Bill was ready for introduction in January 1951.[57] ALA and the Public Libraries Division, of course, supported the bill wholeheartedly as did the public library community in general. To secure passage, it was necessary to gain the support of legislators, their constituents, voters' groups, and other groups as well. Such support could best be gained by maximizing the contribution of the public library to American society. To anyone in the public library community who favored federal and state aid, it must have seemed that this was hardly the time to carry on an acrimonious debate over whether or not the public library should concentrate on serving a small minority of well-educated, middle-class users.

Another circumstance favored silence. During 1950, leaders of the public library community were preparing for the seventy-fifth anniversary of ALA in 1951. By July 1950, the ALA leadership had decided that the theme for the following year's "celebration" would be "the American heritage in terms of present day crises."[58] In conjuction with the celebration, a national program was designed to encourage reading and discussion in order to "influence in a very useful manner the thinking of the American public on the very crucial problems facing us."[59] The Fund for Adult Education of the Ford Foundation provided $150,000 to support the program for one year. The fund was "anxious to have the adult discussion program on the American Heritage as widespread as possible. . . . Renewal and possible increase of the grant will depend upon the showing made this year."[60] A discussion of the inquiry preceding or during the celebration and program would certainly have hit a sour and discouraging note. The American Heritage Program, like the Great Issues Program a few years earlier, was for the political education of the masses. A main point of the inquiry was that the library cannot contribute significantly to such political education. A discussion of the inquiry could hardly fail to highlight that point. Such a discussion was likely to dampen enthusiasm for the anniversary celebration and the American Heritage Program and might imperil the support of the Fund for Adult Education.

Thus there were many reasons for the public library community as a whole to favor or tolerate silence on the Public Library Inquiry; and silence there was. But there was a problem.

If the inquiry was to be successfully ignored, serious discussions of the purpose for the public library had to be avoided. The inquiry was the most thorough and authoritative study of the public library ever carried out. The inquiry had taken a definite and amply justified position on purpose. Any discussion of purpose that left the inquiry's position out of account would not be a serious discussion. Serious discussions could not ignore the most authoritative positon on the issue. The decision to ignore the inquiry, there-fore, made it impossible for the public library community to treat seriously the matter of purpose.

But the matter of purpose could not be avoided altogether for very long. It was bound to come up, for example, in connection with the Library Service Bill. If the public library community was to continue to ignore the inquiry, then the subject of purpose, when it did come up, could not be treated seriously. It would have to be treated some other way, some way that was not serious. That was the price of ignoring the Public Library Inquiry.

NOTES

1. Bernard Berelson, *The Library's Public* (New York: Columbia University Press, 1949), 10.
2. Ibid., 101.
3. Ibid., 85.
4. Ibid., 71.
5. Ibid., 86.
6. Ibid., 49–50.
7. Ibid., 87.
8. Ibid., 85.
9. Ibid., 130–31.
10. Ibid., 131–32.
11. Robert D. Leigh, *The Public Library in the United States* (New York: Columbia University Press, 1950), 16–18.
12. Ibid., 19.
13. Ibid., 15.
14. Ibid., 23.
15. Ibid., 24.
16. Ibid., 39.
17. Ibid., 46.
18. Ibid., 48–50.
19. Ibid., 50–52.
20. *A Forum on the Public Library Inquiry: The Conference at the University of Chicago Graduate Library School, August 8–13, 1949*, ed. Lester Asheim (New York: Columbia University Press, 1950), 37.
21. Ibid., 42–44.
22. Ibid., 45.

23. Ibid., 46.

24. Ibid., 48.

25. Ibid.

26. Ibid., 60.

27. Ibid., 61–62.

28. Ibid., 256.

29. Ibid., 259.

30. Ibid., 270–71.

31. Ibid., 272–76.

32. R. Keith Doms, "Conference Highlights," *ALA Bulletin* 43 (December 1949): 362.

33. Karl Brown, "Middle Atlantic States Regional ALA Conference," *ALA Bulletin* 43 (December 1949): 373.

34. Ruth Gregory, "Conference Review," *ALA Bulletin* 43 (December 1949): 371.

35. Eugene H. Wilson, "Conference Highlights," *ALA Bulletin* 43 (October 1949): 300.

36. Ruth Hale Gershevsky, "Conference Action," *ALA Bulletin* 43 (October 1949): 298–99; John Mackenzie Cory, "Memo to Members," *ALA Bulletin* 43 (September 1949): 261.

37. "The Public Library Inquiry," *Public Libraries* 3 (December 1949): 42.

38. Raymond C. Lindquist, "If Not the People's University, Then What?" *Public Libraries* 3 (March 1950): 3.

39. Emerson Greenaway, "Setting the Course for the Next Decade,"*Public Libraries* 3 (March 1950): 9–13.

40. Ralph A. Ulveling, "Moving Forward . . . As the People's University," *Public Libraries* 3 (March 1950): 13–16.

41. American Library Association, *Proceedings of the 69th Annual Conference, Cleveland, July 16–22, 1950* (Chicago: American Library Association, 1950), 54.

42. Gretchen Knief Schenk, "The Public Library Inquiry," *Library Journal* 76 (March 1, 1951): 373.

43. Gertrude Gscheidle, "Implications of the Public Library Inquiry for the State of Illinois," *ILA Record* 3 (December 1949): 30.

44. John Mackenzie Cory, "The Public Library Inquiry," *Arkansas Libraries* 6 (January 1950): 15–21.

45. Helen Luce, "Public Objects to Libraries' Dropping Fiction," *Library Journal* 75 (May 1, 1950): 765.

46. Edwin Castagna, "First California Returns on the Public Library Inquiry," *Library Journal* 75 (May 1, 1950): 741–44.

47. Edward B. Hayward, "A Positive Approach to *The Library's Public*," *Wisconsin Library Bulletin* 46 (October 1950): 3–4, 32.

48. Margaret E. Davidson, "The PLI and You," *Iowa Library Quarterly* 16 (October 1950): 99–104.

49. Eli Oboler, "The Elite and the Public Library," *Library Journal 75 (August 1950): 1283–84.*

50. *Margaret Paulus, "Why Not Recreation?" Library Journal* 75 (September 15, 1950): 1481–84.

51. John F. Carroll, "Questions Effectiveness of Public Library Inquiry," *Library Journal* 75 (October 1, 1950): 1534, 1536.

52. Robert E. Kingery, Letter, *Library Journal* 75 (November 15, 1950): 1928.

53. Ralph Munn, "Public Library Objectives in 1950," *Public Libraries* 4 (October 1950): 54–57.

54. John Mackenzie Cory, "Memo to Members," *ALA Bulletin* 44 (November 1950): 382.

55. Frances M. Postell, Letter, *Wilson Library Bulletin* 25 (March 1951): 484–85.

56. "Informal LJ Survey," *Library Journal* 76 (October 15, 1951): 1588.

57. Margie S. Malmberg, "The Library Service Bill," *Public Libraries* 5 (February 1951): 4.

58. Ralph E. Ellsworth, "ALA Seventy-fifth Anniversary Celebration," *ALA Bulletin* 44 (September 1950): 309.

59. Sallie J. Farrell, "The Challenge," *ALA Bulletin* 45 (April 1951): 136.

60. Grace T. Stevenson, "ALA's New Project," *ALA Bulletin* 45 (October 1951): 302.

6

Folklore and Public Relations

1950–1965

The early 1950s were exciting times for librarians. Prospects for federal aid for library extension were encouraging. The American Heritage Program had been successfully launched and received generous and continuing support from the Fund for Adult Education. Some of the excitement, however, was mixed with trouble and anxiety. There was a war in Korea; at home anti-communist fervor and fear of subversion were rampant.

The Korean War began in the summer of 1950. Before the end of the year, the Chinese intervened. At first, it seemed that public libraries might mobilize for another war effort, this time with emphasis on civilian defense against atomic attack. In April 1951, descriptions of civilian defense programs at the Brooklyn, Detroit, and Louisville public libraries were published in the *ALA Bulletin*. The programs featured films such as "Pattern for Survival" and "You Can Beat the A-Bomb." There was concern, in Brooklyn at least, "that atomic attack might come at any moment and find the city's millions utterly unprepared."[1] The *ALA Bulletin* promised to publish accounts of what other libraries were doing to meet their responsibilities in the "national emergency"; but the stories never appeared. The attention of librarians was drawn to other matters.

The fear of communism and the outrages to civil liberties and common sense produced by that fear, was of more immediate concern to librarians than the Korean War and the threat of atomic attack. The anticommunist crusade involved librarians as combatants.

In 1949 and 1950, events pushed American fear and hatred of communism to the point of hysteria. In 1949, Russia exploded an atomic bomb. Americans were told that spies in government, from the White House on down, had made the Russian bomb possible. That same year, Chinese communists established control over China. In February 1950, a British scientist was arrested for giving atomic secrets to the Russians. In the spring of 1950,

Congress held hearings on communist influence in the State Department. In June, South Korea was invaded. Later that Summer, the Rosenbergs were arrested for spying. In December, American troops were in full retreat from Chinese invaders. Americans were understandably alarmed when, in January 1951, J. Edgar Hoover warned them that half a million communists and fellow-travelers in the United States were ready to work destruction in the event of war with Russia. The following month, the junior senator from Wisconsin showed a West Virginia audience a paper bearing, he said, the names of 205 subversives working in the State Department. The McCarthy era had begun.[2]

Throughout the period of hysteria, librarians were targets of the anticommunist crusaders. In March 1950, Elizabeth Haas of the Enoch Pratt Free Library was fired for refusing to take a loyalty oath. In July, Ruth Brown, librarian at Bartlesville, Oklahoma, for thirty years, was fired. She was accused of buying subversive periodicals including *The Nation* and *The New Republic*. In 1951, patriotic groups pressured librarians to label materials sympathetic to communism. The Intellectual Freedom Committee was asked to adopt a labeling plan. The committee responded with a strong statement against labeling that was adopted by the ALA Council in July 1951. In 1952, a Boston newspaper accused the Boston Public Library of promoting communist materials. That same year, Senator McCarthy announced that overseas libraries maintained by the State Department contained "30,000 dangerous books" by 418 "suspect" authors including Edna Ferber, Dashiel Hammett, and Stephen Vincent Benet.[3] The State Department ordered the removal of some books; and a few were burned. The press and President Eisenhower denounced book-burning. In June 1953, ALA issued the *Freedom to Read* statement asserting that librarians were "guardians of the people's freedom to read" and must "contest encroachments upon that freedom."[4] In 1955, a state American Legion publication identified ALA as a Red front. That same year, Senator McCarthy identified the Fund for the Republic, a contributor to the Committee on Intellectual Freedom, as a "vicious communist propaganda machine."[5] One can readily see what ALA leaders had in mind when they selected the theme for the 1951 anniversary celebration: The Heritage of the United States in Times of Crisis.

The American Heritage Project, the name given the program conceived in conjunction with the anniversary celebration, began in earnest in the fall of 1951. A project office was opened; meetings were held; plans were made to provide training for discussion leaders; and lists of books and films were compiled. By January 1952, the discussions had begun in selected demonstration areas where discussion leaders and project officials could experiment and learn from experience. By the time the program was a year old, 117 discussion groups were meeting.

American Heritage discussion groups typically met from six to twelve times a year. All members were supposed to have read the same selection.

Readings included the *Declaration of Independence* and other documents from American history and books with such titles as *This I Do Believe, USA: A Permanent Revolution*, and *Living Ideas in America*. From 1951 until 1957, when the American Heritage Project ended, 1,474 groups involving 28,476 persons met in "more than 300 communities in 33 states."[6] The smallest number of members, 2,439, participated the first year. The peak year was 1953–54 when 6,917 members were involved.[7] During the course of the program, the Fund for Adult Education gave ALA $750,000 for its support.[8]

While the American Heritage Project was taking shape in 1951, the public library community was launching a campaign to secure passage of the Library Services Bill. The bill called for federal grants totaling $7.5 million annually for five years. The bill was designed "to stimulate states to strengthen existing but inadequate services and to extend library service primarily to rural areas." The states were to receive grants based in part on the relative size of the rural population and were then required to provide funds based on per capita income. State libraries were to administer the funds which were to be used primarily for demonstration libraries, bookmobiles, advisory services, and books for state libraries.[9] The *ALA Bulletin* indicated the "need for the bill." "The average American spends less than nine years in school. Some concerted effort must be made to help him continue his education during the remaining years of his life. . . . Rural boys and girls are getting an inferior education. Since Korea, over 300,000 men, unable to meet the educational requirements of Selective Service, have been rejected for military service." Although the bill provides mainly for rural areas, the cities should support the bill because of the "migration of . . . rural youth to urban areas. . . . The urban citizen cannot ignore the educational needs of the farmer."[10] By January 1952, sixteen national organizations were supporting the bill, including the National Education Association, AMVETS, the United Auto Workers, the American Association of University Women, the PTA, and the Grange.

Congress adjourned in August 1952 without taking action on the bill. The 83d Congress (1953–54) also failed to take action. Both the House and Senate "held up all legislation which dealt with federal grants in aid to education. Their reason for doing this was anticipation of a report on the role of the federal governmnent in education." The report, published in June 1955, acknowledged the educational importance of public libraries, but said they were a state and local responsibility; no "compelling national interest" justified federal action.[11]

The library profession did not agree. The vigorous effort on behalf of the bill continued. Support in Congress had grown over the previous two years. Librarians had learned the art of lobbying.

Hearings on the bill were held in May 1955. A political scientist from the University of Illinois was much impressed with

the competence of the library profession in lobbying and in deploying political forces in a competitive situation. . . . The preparation and briefing of witnesses had been worked out to the last possible degree. The persons chosen were chosen magnificently well to represent a particular segment of society . . . to appeal to the members of Congress . . . as exponents and representatives of very highly cherished interests in American life.[12]

The hearings were held May 25–27, 1955, Of the forty witnesses who appeared, only one opposed the bill—the U.S. Commissioner of Education who represented the administration. Of the other witnesses, ten were congressmen, and fifteen were representatives of various organizations and social groups such as farmers, business executives, students, parents, educational institutions, and so on. A clergyman and a newspaper editor also appeared. Two public librarians testified: the director of the Rochester, New York, Public Library and the director of the Seattle Public Library who was also president-elect of ALA. The Librarian of Congress also testified on behalf of the bill.

Testimony in favor of the bill emphasized two points: the inadequacy of public library service and the educational importance of the public library. On the first point, John Richards, director of the Seattle Public Library and ALA president-elect, testified that 27 million people had no public library service; and only a small minority of Americans had minimally adequate service. Richards offered many facts and figures in support of his testimony which was corroborated by many of the witnesses. Testimony concerning the educational importance of libraries consisted primarily of what Ralph Munn had called folklore in his summary of the 1949 conference on the Public Library Inquiry. An officer of the ALA Trustees' Section stated that "libraries are second only to schools in their capacity to educate our citizens."[13] A congressman from New Jersey stated that for those over eighteen years of age

the free public library assumes an increasingly large role. . . . In our ever-increasingly complex society, we must have well-educated citizens with a real understanding of the issues facing their country and the world if our democracy is to survive. Our free public libraries provide a ready medium for continuing our citizens' education beyond their formal school years. . . . They provide a ready forum for the development of an intelligent understanding of our local, State, national and international issues.[14]

L. Quincy Mumford, the Librarian of Congress, testified that "for most people the public library is the chief—and sometimes the only—means of carrying on their education after they leave school. It is the adjunct of our free public school system and as such is vital to the maintenance of the American tradition of independent thought and action."[15] John Richards testified as follows:

The public library, of course, is the one opportunity for all adults . . . to carry on continuing education throughout life. . . . Where libraries are available people are making continuous use of them. The use of libraries for informational purposes has grown tremendously in recent years. The well-stocked library is rapidly becoming the first source the citizen uses when he needs help in the solution of his day-to-day problems or when he needs to get an understanding of the complex world in which he lives. . . . The public library is such a source and is being used increasingly in this connection. . . . Libraries are a necessity if we are to keep our citizens informed and ready to take their part in the democratic kind of government which we all approve and enjoy.[16]

The campaign on behalf of the Library Services Bill represented the public library as an important agency for the education and political enlightenment of the people. The bill was passed the following year. The Library Services Act was signed into law on June 19, 1956.

At the ALA conference that same month, the ALA Council adopted a new set of standards for public libraries presented in a document entitled *Public Library Service*. A committee of the Public Libraries Division had recommended the creation of new standards and had been working on them since 1954. The standards were necessary, said the committee, because the 1943 standards were out of date; there was a need to incorporate "the concept of systems . . . an idea presented in the Public Library Inquiry . . . and now appearing in state plans."[17] The 1956 standards were designed as standards for public library systems.

Leigh's general report of the Public Library Inquiry had indeed recommended the creation of "larger public library systems by consolidation, federation, or voluntary association" and "federal grants of modest amounts in aid of specified state programs for building larger library units."[18] Many state plans in preparation as early as 1952 envisioned library systems.[19] But the systems recommended by the inquiry were to enable the public library to provide improved and distinctive services for the library's natural audience, the minority of adults who possessed the interest, will, and ability to seek such services. The 1956 standards were designed to promote the creation of systems, but not for the purpose intended by the inquiry. How then were the standards to represent the purpose for the systems?

The introductory statement to the standards in which one would expect to find a statement of purpose was entitled "The Role of the Public Library." It was written not by a librarian, but by a journalist and long-time promoter of library causes, Gerald W. Johnson. Johnson provided a glowing account of the library as an important agency of popular education and political enlightenment. The "function" of the public library, he said, "is the function of an open door. The public library is a way of escape from the narrow area of our individual lives into the field, finite, no doubt, but unbounded, of the wisdom and experience of all mankind. It is not only the way of escape, but for the majority of us it is by far the widest and the easiest to pass through."[20] The position of the United States as a world leader added to the importance of the library:

There is the most urgent need for our people to broaden their intellectual horizon with all possible speed, for the moment of crisis is already upon us. . . . We cannot become a nation of philosophers; but we can become a nation aware of the existence of philosophy and respectful of its findings. Indeed, we face the grim necessity of becoming just that, or of failing in our great task of world leadership. . . . For the overwhelming majority, the quickest and easiest access to the world's best thought is through the public library. To maintain this source of information open to all . . . is a task important beyond all computation, not just to ourselves alone but to the world.[21]

Some librarians and some communities were not meeting their responsibilities, Johnson said. Some librarians failed to make the library "magnetic"; some communities did not support the library. But in a community where librarians and the public acted as they should, "there one finds a community in which American civilization is coming into flower."[22]

In addition to Johnson's essay, the standards provided other statements concerning the purpose for the library. The first chapter, entitled "Functions of the Public Library," stated that the library provided materials in order

to facilitate informal self-education of all people in the community, to enrich and further develop the subjects on which individuals are undertaking formal education, to meet the informational needs of all, to support the educational, civic and cultural activities of groups and organizations, to encourage wholesome recreation and constructive use of leisure time.[23]

Midway through the volume, in a chapter entitled "Books and Nonbook Materials," another statement declared that the library's "function" was to provide materials that help "all people" to

educate themselves continuously, keep pace with progress in all fields of knowledge, become better members of home and community, discharge political and social obligations, be more capable in their daily occupations, develop their creative and spiritual capacities, appreciate and enjoy works of art and literature, make such use of leisure time as will promote personal and social well-being, contribute to the growth of knowledge.[24]

The latter statement was an edited version of the "objectives" stated in the National Plans of the 1930s and the standards of 1943 and included in the report of the Public Library Inquiry. Both of the statements that appeared in the text of the standards were given without argument or interpretation. There was no hint that anyone ever seriously suggested that these "functions" coincide with the interests, volition, and ability of relatively few people.

The 1956 standards disclosed how those responsible for them dealt with the problem mentioned in the last chapter, that of treating the matter of purpose while continuing to ignore the Public Library Inquiry. For the introduction, which called for a formal and extended essay on purpose, those responsible for the standards engaged an outsider to write a public relations article. Elsewhere in the standards, traditional statements of purpose were presented without argument or explanation. The treatment of purpose offered in the standards consisted of public relations and gratuitous assertion that pretended to be unaware of any difficulty.

During the 1950s, the public library community was more concerned with public relations than ever before. Commentators on the Public Library Inquiry maintained that public relations was the solution to the problem of enlarging the library's public. The campaign to secure passage of the Library Services Act involved a vigorous public relations campaign. Throughout the decade, public relations was a favorite topic in library publications. When National Library Week was launched in 1958, the president of ALA called it "our year round long-range educational program of public relations for libraries."[25] The theme of the public relations enterprise was repeated consistently and often: The public library was for everyone; the library was vitally important for the intellectual and political well-being of the American people.

In the 1950s, the public library community, frightened and demoralized by the Public Library Inquiry, would not argue that position in a serious way; so it relied on publicity and salesmanship to make the point. There was no lack of awareness that the Public Library Inquiry was a threat to public relations. At the 1959 ALA midwinter meeting, Emerson Greenaway, ALA president and chairman of National Library Week, gave a speech to state directors of the upcoming NLW campaign. "Let us remind ourselves," Greenaway said, "of the necessity of overcoming any lingering thought we may still have that libraries, their materials and services, are for those who seek them out of their own accord." The reference to the library's natural audience identified in Leigh's inquiry report was obvious. The library, Greenaway continued, was "a vital center of ideas and information, related to everybody's life and interest." That idea "must still be 'sold' to a great majority of the population."[26] It was sometimes necessary to admit the truth when urging librarians to do their public relations duty. An eminent authority, recommending public relations in a speech entitled "Public Relations Specifics for the 1960s," reminded his audience that "to a greater extent than any of us likes to admit, it is still true that most of the library's effort in most communities goes to serve the somewhat marginal needs of a rather small minority of citizens."[27]

While the public relations enterprise was flourishing in the late 1950's, the money made available by the Library Services Act was making its way around the country. By early 1957, a few states were receiving checks from Washington. By late 1957, forty-six state plans had been approved. Those plans had a total budget of $14,220,925. About 31 percent of that was federal money; the rest was state and local.

Over the next three years, bookmobiles appeared on country roads; state libraries were improved; and county and regional libraries were established. After the Library Services Act had been in effect four years, its results were pronounced "impressive: 34 million rural people now have new or improved services.... State funds... have increased 75 per cent.... Local appropriations for rural libraries have increased 50 per cent.... Approximately 250 new bookmobiles are now operating.... Over 1½ million rural children and adults have service for the first time."[28]

The bookmobile was the centerpiece; bookmobile service "comprised the largest single activity in the LSA program." By "a conservative estimate... one-third of the federal and state money" was spent on bookmobile service.[29] Public relations literature featured bookmobile stories, tales of "the motor-driven library which opens so wide a door between these little stopping places in the hills and the great world of thought and beauty and imagination."[30]

Testimonials from the states proclaimed the benefits of the Library Services Act. A demonstration library in Virginia made an influential citizen enthusiastic about paying taxes. People in Oklahoma left their storm cellars to greet the bookmobile. In a Montana town, the marshal and ranch hands became readers. A woman in Texas regularly drove ninety miles to meet the bookmobile. Many states reported a new attitude in rural towns:

The fact that the federal government believes in the necessity of public library service as a safeguard to democratic government and is backing the belief with hard cash has been convincing proof to many local appropriating bodies of necessity for more local funds for the same purpose.[31]

A public relations book about the Library Services Act concluded as follows:

Taken as a whole... the results that have been attained from the Library Services Act have been of almost immeasurable value.... One accomplishment in particular... far surpasses all its other gains. Because of this greatly constructive piece of legislation, Americans from coast to coast have been brought to understand both the need for and the value of libraries for everyone, and this, in turn, is certain to make us better citizens not only of America but also of the world.[32]

Only a few professionals were willing to talk seriously about the Library Services Act in public. A few of these appeared at a conference on the act conducted in late 1961 by the U.S. Office of Education and the University of Illinois library school. One of the participants, Lowell Martin, said that there were some "solemn questions."

Martin's main concern was that most of the money generated by the federal program was being used to provide "substandard" service. "We are ... putting our time and money into taking fragmented library service out to people."[33] The 1956 standards were playing a minor role in the library extension program. The poor quality service provided by weak village libraries was being duplicated by poor-quality service provided by bookmobiles and weak county libraries. Martin was more impressed by the accomplishments of some of the strengthened state libraries. He concluded his contribution with an appeal for rededication to national standards and a call for attention to the quality of library service.

Harold Lancour, dean of the library school at the University of Pittsburgh, indicated in his summary of the conference that some participants had "nagging doubts about what *really* had taken place during the last five years":

Someone asked, "Have we gained only superficial results during the past five years?" To be sure, 288 new bookmobiles sounded very impressive and could be proudly described. But as someone said, "288 bookmobiles for what?" . . . to bring substandard library service to local areas. . . . There was a great deal of talk about demonstration libraries. . . . What happened to a disquieting number of the demonstration libraries? It was discovered that when the time came for the people in the area to take the libraries over, they didn't. They simply weren't willing to spend their own money to do it.[34]

But the solemn questions of the conference hardly reached beyond it. For the public library community at large, the Library Services Act was a spectacular success.

Meanwhile, money from another source was being spent in an effort to strengthen adult education programs in libraries. The Fund for Adult Education, which had supported the American Heritage Project, provided substantial grants to support other adult education projects. Between 1953 and 1961, ALA received $104,500 to maintain an Adult Education Office that administered grants and provided other support for adult education activities. The Fund also provided $500,000 for the Library-Community Project, created to find "methods of developing long range planning of adult education programs."[35] The Library-Community Project lasted from 1955 through 1960. The project conducted workshops and adult education demonstrations.

In 1960, the Library-Community Project issued a small book entitled *Studying the Community*. The authors urged the importance of community study which, they said, was "essential to a reasonable fulfillment" of the library's educational purpose.[36] The recommended community studies were to be carried out by examining published materials, conducting interviews, and distributing questionnaires to library users, local organizations, churches, and samples of the general population. Like other advocates of community study, the authors failed to consider key assumptions which, if invalid, negated the value of such studies. These assumptions were: that there were distinctive, unknown local needs for education that a study would disclose; that, once disclosed, the library was capable of providing materials and programs that responded to those needs; and, the most dubious assumption, that the people who had the needs also had the desire and ability to use the materials and programs made available. The history of adult education in the library suggests that at least two, and perhaps all of those assumptions, were unwarranted.

Studying the Community was a badly organized and shallow piece of work, the result, no doubt, of trying to write about adult education and the library at a time when librarians in general, and especially those in official positions, could not seriously discuss the purpose for the public library.

An evaluation of public library programs supported by the Fund for Adult Education at a cost of $1.3 million was written by a staff member of the Detroit Public Library under the supervision of the chief of the ALA Office for Adult Education. The evaluation concluded that the grant program "made a genuine contribution to the development of continuing liberal education for adults as an established part of community life."[37] In the early 1960s, the Ford Foundation "closed out" the Fund for Adult Education for having been "less than successful."[38] In 1964, ALA closed the Office for Adult Education.

In the early 1960s, a number of developments steered the interest of the public library community away from the exhausted adult education movement. These were the embryonic stages of what was to make the later 1960s so memorable. The early 1960s saw great censorship battles over Henry Miller's novels, *Fanny Hill*, and other books—battles that were among the omens of the coming sexual revolution. Librarians watched with interest and took sides. In 1960, the word *integration* appeared for the first time in *Library Journal's* index. A December 15 editorial urged librarians to get involved in the civil rights movement. And, by 1962 hordes of high school students were invading public libraries, taking all the seats and threatening to wear out the bound volumes of periodicals. Some librarians would not let students use the library at night; others found it strange that public librarians were complaining about an overload of users. The student problem received special attention at the 1963 ALA conference. Before the end of the decade, the students had graduated and were causing trouble elsewhere.

Another important development that caught the attention of the public library community early in the decade was the growing disposition of the government to spend money as it never had before. In 1957, Americans had been shocked when the Russians launched a small satellite known as sputnik. Believing, apparently, that the Russian success signified deficiencies in American education, Congress, in 1958, passed the National Defense Education Act. Title III of the act authorized matching grants for the purchase of educational equipment and materials including books. The purchases were to support instruction in science, mathematics, and foreign languages in public elementary and secondary schools and junior colleges. Title III was expected to make about $125 million available. At the time, annual national expenditures for school libraries was estimated at less than $25 million. Although it was likely that, initially, much of the money would be spent on lab equipment, it also seemed that "so large a sum" would also make possible "a tremendous increase in the holdings of school libraries." It was understood by publishers and, no doubt, by librarians that the Act was "extremely important . . . because of the precedents it may establish for the future pattern of federal aid to education."[39]

In January 1959, a document entitled "Federal Legislative Policy of the American Library Association" was adopted by council. The document called for aid to school, college and university and public libraries. In reference to the latter, the document stated:

The public library is a vital part of our total educational structure and supplements the program of formal education at all levels. The success of the Library Services Act clearly demonstrates the value of federal stimulation grants to improve library service. The Association recommends that federal assistance be provided to the states to stimulate public library development, not only in areas having less than ten thousand population, but also in all areas where library service and facilities are below standard or do not now exist.[40]

In 1960, the Library Services Act was extended for an additional five years. In 1962, an amendment to the Library Services Act was introduced in the House of Representatives. The amendment proposed that federal aid to public libraries no longer be restricted to rural areas and that a great deal more money be provided. "Suddenly," said an editorial in *Library Journal*, "the vision of $70 million in federal aid for libraries was before us."[41]

In January 1963, in his education message to Congress, President Kennedy recommended grants for "urban as well as rural libraries and for construction as well as operation."[42] Kennedy was murdered four days before the legislation was passed in the Senate. On February 11, 1964, President Johnson signed the bill amending the Library Services Act, thereafter known as the Library Services and Construction Act. The first appropriation authorized $55 million—$25 million for services and $30 million for construction. There was more to come. Lyndon Johnson's vision of the Great Society included libraries.

Johnson's first State of the Union message contained his vision:

Let this session of Congress be known as the session . . . which declared all-out war on human poverty and unemployment . . . which finally recognized the health needs of all our older citizens . . . which reformed our tangled transportation and transit policies . . . which achieved the most effective, efficient foreign aid program ever; and as the session which helped to build more homes, more schools, more libraries and more hospitals than any single session of Congress in the history of our Republic.[43]

The June 1964 issue of the *Wilson Library Bulletin* carried a message from Sargent Shriver, a special assistant to President Johnson, calling on librarians to join in the war on poverty:

It is commonly believed that the poor, coming out of deprived backgrounds with little culture and learning, are not motivated toward books and learning. This is a myth which you can help to overcome. . . . American libraries have a key role to play in the war against poverty.[44]

The public library community was willing. The Public Library Inquiry, so long ignored, seemed altogether forgotten. The September 15, 1964, issue of *Library Journal* was devoted to the contribution libraries could make to the war on poverty. An article contributed by Hubert Humphrey entitled "A Spiritual Quest," reminded librarians that "next to our schools, our public libraries are potentially more important in the war on poverty than any other of our public institutions."[45] ALA president, Edwin Castagna, wrote that overcoming the myth that the poor are not motivated by books and learning "is a major mission of public librarians of the United States."[46] Several articles described public library work in progress among the poor.

In January 1965, the *ALA Bulletin* listed war-on-poverty programs applicable to libraries and indicated the kinds of programs that might qualify for money. The Economic Opportunity Act of 1964 offered many possibilities:

Hours of service of libraries in deprived areas can be increased; employing and training staff for projects to serve the undereducated and culturally deprived children, young adults and adults can be funded. . . . Programs in literacy, vocational information, consumer guidance homemaking and child-rearing skills can qualify.

Research and demonstration projects seeking "effective ways of reaching the disadvantaged" could also qualify.[47]

In May 1965, a well-known psychologist, Kenneth B. Clark, issued a note of warning at a Conference on Librarians, Books and the Poverty Program held at Pratt Institute. Clark said that the poor were too badly educated to profit from books. Until the education of the poor improved, libraries would not be relevant to poverty programs. Clark hoped that librarians would not create programs that amounted to a "cruel hoax" on the poor. "The war on poverty," he said, "cannot be waged in terms of public relations, promises and verbal concern." Clark's audience did not appreciate his warning.[48]

Because of the "increasing interest of the federal government in libraries . . . and other developments of the mid–1960s," the Public Library Association of ALA decided to revise the standards of 1956.[49] A new set entitled *Minimum Standards for Public Library Systems* was approved in July 1966. A statement of purpose to introduce the standards was necessary; but the leaders of the public library community responsible for such a statement had nothing to say. They dusted off the old essay by Gerald W. Johnson from the 1956 standards and reprinted it as an introduction to the new set.

In 1966, it appeared that the public library community had reason to congratulate itself for refusing to get involved in serious and controversial discussions about the place of the public library in American society. The record of the last fifteen years spoke for itself. Folklore and public relations had delivered the Library Services Act and a small fortune from the Fund for Adult Education. The Library Services and Construction Act and Lyndon Johnson's Great Society program seemed to mark the beginning of a prosperity librarians had never before known. Folklore and public relations supplemented by expert lobbying made a winning combination.

NOTES

1. "Libraries Lead the Way in Civilian Defense," *ALA Bulletin* 45 (April 1951): 128.

2. See David M. Oshinsky, *A Conspiracy So Immense: The World of Joe McCarthy* (New York: Free Press, 1983).

3. Claudia Perry-Holmes, "Censorship and Libraries: A Look Back at the 'Fifties'," *Newsletter on Intellectual Freedom* 32 (May 1983): 93.

4. "The Freedom to Read," *ALA Bulletin* 47 (November 1953): 482.

5. Dennis Thomison, *A History of the American Library Association* (Chicago: American Library Association, 1978), 190.

6. Charles H. Hewitt, *Grant Evaluation Study* (Chicago: American Library Association, 1958), 132.

7. Ibid., 53.

8. Ibid., 180.

9. "Knowledge is Power: A Summary of the Library Services Bill," *ALA Bulletin* 46 (January 1952): 21.

10. Ibid., 23.

11. Germaine Krettek, "LSA, the Federal Government, and the Profession," in *The Impact of the Library Services Act: Progress and Potential* (Champaign: University of Illinois Graduate School of Library Science, 1962), 22.

12. Philip Monypenny, "LSA: A Political Scientist's View," in *The Impact of the Library Services Act*, 97.

13. U.S. Congress. House Committee on Education and Labor. Subcommittee on Federal Aid for Library Service in Rural Areas. *Hearings Held at Washington, D.C., May 25, 26, 27, 1955* (Washington: Government Printing Office, 1955), 116.

14. Ibid., 129–30.

15. Ibid., 85.

16. Ibid., 23, 34.

17. "Revising Post-War Standards," *Public Libraries* 8 (March 1954): 1.

18. Robert D. Leigh, *The Public Library in the United States* (New York: Columbia University Press, 1950), 229–30.

19. S. Janice Key, "The States' Responsibility for Public Library Services," *Public Libraries* 6 (November 1952): 89.

20. *Public Library Service: A Guide to Evaluation with Minimum Standards* (Chicago: American Library Association, 1956), ix.

21. Ibid., x-xi.

22. Ibid., xii.

23. Ibid., 4.

24. Ibid., 31.

25. Emerson Greenaway, Editorial, *ALA Bulletin* 53 (March 1959): 189.

26. Ibid.

27. Dan Lacy, "Public Relations Specifics for the 1960's," *ALA Bulletin* 55 (June 1961): 559.

28. John G. Lorenz and Herbert A. Carl, "The Library Services Act after Four Years," *ALA Bulletin* 55 (June 1961): 534.

29. Lowell A. Martin, "LSA and Library Standards: Two Sides of the Coin," in *The Impact of the Library Services Act*, 7.

30. Hawthorne Daniel, *Public Libraries for Everyone* (Garden City, N.Y.: Doubleday, 1961), 168.

31. Lorenz and Carl, "The Library Services Act after Four Years," 536-40.

32. Daniel, *Public Libraries for Everyone*, 180-81.

33. Martin, "LSA and Library Standards," 7.

34. Harold Lancour, "Summary," in *The Impact of the Library Services Act*, 116-17.

35. Hewitt, *Grant Evaluation Study*, 180.

36. ALA Library-Community Project, *Studying the Community* (Chicago: American Library Association, 1960), 2.

37. Hewitt, *Grant Evaluation Study*, 178.

38. Fred Harvey Harrington, *The Future of Adult Education* (San Francisco: Jossey-Bass, 1977), 24.

39. Dan Lacy, "National Defense Education Act of 1958," *Library Journal* 84 (February 15, 1959): 569-70.

40. "Federal Legislative Policy of the American Library Association," *ALA Bulletin* 53 (April 1959): 281-82.

41. Editorial, *Library Journal* 87 (December 15, 1962): 4500.

42. Edward G. Holley and Robert F. Schremser, *The Library Services and Construction Act* (Greenwich, Conn.: Jai Press, 1983), 59.

43. Ibid., 69-70.

44. Sargent Shriver, "A Message of American Librarians," *Wilson Library Bulletin* 38 (June 1964): 833.

45. Hubert H. Humphrey, "A Spiritual Quest," *Library Journal* 89 (September 15, 1964): 3243.

46. Edwin Castagna, "To Overcome the Myth," *Library Journal* 89 (September 15, 1964): 3251.

47. Pauline Winnick, "Libraries and the War on Poverty: Relevant Federal Legislative Programs," *ALA Bulletin* 59 (January 1965): 46.

48. Editorial, *Library Journal* 90 (June 15, 1965): 2772.

49. *Minimum Standards for Public Library Systems, 1966* (Chicago: American Library Association, 1967), vi.

7

Information for the People

1965–1980

The 1966 standards were obsolete when they were published. The view of the public library's role presented in the introduction to the standards was even more so. By 1966, the country was in the early stages of a populist social movement that was to grow stronger as the decade continued and was to culminate in a period of turbulence and conflict that permanently changed the attitudes and values of Americans and the character of American social institutions.

The public library could not isolate itself from the social movement of the time or the turbulence and changes it wrought. Many librarians believed that the public library was obliged to get involved in the populist social movement and help to realize its vision of a new American society, free of oppression and inequality. Other librarians, less disposed to populist enthusiasm, believed that the public library must adjust to the situation created by the populist movement. The library must establish its identity as an institution serving all the people. The library must create new forms of service that would make it a vital force in the life of the community as a whole. If the library could not become an authentic popular institution, its political and financial support would evaporate in the new populist era. Thus, for more than a decade, public librarians, moved by populist idealism or fear of financial disaster or both, tried to transform the the public library into something it had never been. That effort is the subject of this chapter.

In 1965, the groundwork for a period of social change was in place. Postwar babies were nearly grown up. In Southeast Asia, a crisis in cold war politics was imminent. At home, the civil rights movement was gathering strength. The Great Society program was beginning its assault on social ills. And a new and mysterious impulse was at work driving people of different kinds and degrees to seek higher levels of autonomy, expression, and gratification, on the one hand, and stronger interpersonal and community bonds, on the other. The events of 1965 signaled the beginning of a strange, new era.

In February, the Viet Cong attacked a barracks at Pleiku where American military advisers were quartered. In March, the first American combat troops went ashore in Vietnam. That same month sheriff's deputies and city police seriously injured more than fifty civil rights marchers in Selma, Alabama. In April, 15,000 young people joined in an antiwar protest organized by a group known as the Students for a Democratic Society. In August, the worst race riot in a generation took place in the Watts section of Los Angeles. In October, students at Berkeley held a Vietnam day demonstration. In 1965, the first study of student drug use was conducted; the word *hippie* was coined by a reporter for the *San Francisco Chronicle*; and a new form of rock music was becoming popular around the country.

For the next few years, it seemed that American society might tear itself apart. Cities, campuses, and households were scenes of constant and bitter conflict as the establishment and its adversaries confronted one another. The war and civil rights were central issues in the conflict; but it ranged beyond those issues into nearly every area of national life. It seemed as if young people, black militants, and assorted allies from many sectors of society were intent on a revolution that would transform government, education, families, the workplace, manners, sexual conduct, and anything else that seemed in need of transformation.

The revolutionary program was to unite all of the oppressed and discontented in a great popular rebellion:

The dream was that the converging rebellions of students, pacifists, draft resisters, black militants, Mexican farm workers, welfare mothers, frustrated suburban housewives, reservation Indians, penitentiary inmates, hippies from the California beaches and the western wilderness, and bored workers on the General Motors assembly lines would all roll together into one millenarian Mississippi of revolution.[1]

The aims of the revolutionaries were not narrowly political or economic; they were indeed millenarian. The revolution was to bring "a higher reason, a more human community, and a new and liberated individual. Its ultimate creation will be a new and enduring wholeness and beauty—a renewed relationship of man to himself, to other men, to society, to nature, and to the land."[2]

Through 1966 and 1967, the revolution seemed to gain strength. In 1968, the country was shaken by violence. Early in April, Martin Luther King was assassinated, precipitating destructive riots in a hundred American cities. In August, police battled young revolutionaries in Chicago during the Democratic National Convention. As the new decade began, however, the revolution was winding down.

There were many reasons. After the Tet offensive early in 1968 revealed unexpected enemy strength, public opinion in the United States began to turn against the war. On that point, the views of the revolutionaries and middle America converged. By 1972, support for the war had nearly evaporated.

Meanwhile, the revolution was cooling because it was succeeding. Universities changed curricula and residence rules, appointed students to governing bodies, and appeared willing to consider every demand and tolerate almost any kind of protest. Government bodies grew tolerant of demonstrations and even of civil disobedience. Institutions of every type became more open, egalitarian, and deferential to popular wishes. Revolutionary dress, music, manners, and language became the fashions of the middle class. The values and attitudes of the revolution penetrated society as a whole. By the time the revolution ended, American society had changed a great deal. A very different country entered the age of Watergate, oil shocks, and inflation.

The revolutionary turmoil of 1965 and 1966 hardly touched the public library community as it planned programs for the war on poverty and projects to be funded by grants authorized by the Library Services and Construction Act. By 1967, however, the ideas and values of the revolution reached the public library community. In his inaugural address at the 1967 conference in San Francisco, the new ALA president spoke of "the strong winds of controversy shaking our political, educational and social fields. . . . Up to now their effect upon our work has been marginal." But this was no longer the case, he said, adding that "some of these cross-currents are being felt directly by our libraries."[3]

The revolution divided the community of professional librarians as it divided other communities. The division was apparent at the 1967 conference. The Adult Services Division of ALA cosponsored a speech by General Maxwell Taylor, former ambassador to South Vietnam. Taylor defended administration policies in Vietnam and received a standing ovation. His speech, however, also provoked a response unheard of at library conventions, a protest demonstration with pickets. Most of the demonstrators were students; but some were librarians. By the end of 1967, it was clear that many librarians were in sympathy with the revolution and were intent upon making the public library a part of it.

Radical or progressive librarians, often called "young activists," envisioned an important role for the public library. The library was to seek out those groups in American society that were powerless, oppressed victims of poverty and discrimination, and work to bring them into the mainstream where they might enjoy the benefits of power and affluence. The groups that were to be the beneficiaries—known collectively as the disadvantaged—were those that traditionally made little or no use of the public library. Librarians who advocated service to the disadvantaged claimed that the library was at fault.

It had never made a serious effort to serve the disadvantaged or reached out with suitable programs. In 1967, a massive effort to serve the disadvantaged began in earnest.

In November 1967, as Conference on Library Service to the Unserved was held at the University of Wisconsin—Milwaukee. Edwin Castagna, director of the Enoch Pratt Free Library, spoke for advocates of service to the disadvantaged:

If as librarians, we do not reach out to all the unserved people within our country during this tortured time of troubles, we will have failed to grasp one of the biggest opportunities libraries have had. If we fail, we will have earned the disdain of our successors, and we will have betrayed our public trust as essential agents in our nation's apparatus for education.[4]

The outreach movement that began in 1967 and lasted about four years was indeed an educational movement; its purpose was to educate the disadvantaged, to turn them into readers of good books. The proponents of outreach in 1967 understood that the work would be difficult and would require innovation and energy. The public library would have to be changed into a place that the disadvantaged would find attractive and comfortable. A new breed of librarian capable of work with the disadvantaged would have to be recruited and trained. And different types of materials would have to be provided: "movies, tape recorders, typewriters and viewmasters . . . a number of different kinds of resources that would lead to the reading of books," said one of the speakers at the 1967 Milwaukee conference.[5] Outreach would begin with new and different facilities, activities, materials, and a new type of librarian. But outreach was traditional. It was to provide education through reading.

Early advocates of outreach were confident. Another speaker at the Milwaukee conference, Eva G. Williams of the New Haven Public Library, exhibited the optimism characteristic at the time:

Let's recognize the concept that poverty is no deterrent to learning or success in life. Cultural deprivation is not necessarily a matter of poverty. . . . The "poor" have the same needs, desires and abilities as we. It is simply a matter of discovery, encouragement, stimulation . . . imparting . . . the knowledge that somebody cares. . . . Are we to be interested in helping people who need it most, to begin where their interests are and with the kind of reading they can do, confident that they will progress? The answer is yes, of course![6]

One of the conference participants, a representative of a "disadvantaged community," had a different view of what might be accomplished by traditional library services in poor neighborhoods: "So, you've got a thousand books on those shelves that you're passing out to kids who can't even read. Now I don't know what you think about it, but I think you are wasting your time. I think the services you are offering are totally irrelevant, and that you are not facing the problem at hand."[7]

But at the time, confidence in the efficacy of traditional services was general among public librarians committed to outreach. In the fall of 1967, the University of Maryland library school started "an experimental project in library education and research in the area of work with the disadvantaged."[8] This was the much publicized "High John" project. The library school developed an educational program and helped to establish a public library in an impoverished black neighborhood near Baltimore. The library was to serve the neighborhood and, at the same time, provide practical experience for students and field experience for researchers. In November 1967, Eric Moon, editor of *Library Journal*, visited High John and talked to Richard Moses, field director of the project. Moon was "impressed by the uniformly high quality of the adult fiction." Moses told him that "even though the library's in a depressed area, you don't have to underestimate people's interest or capacity. Also, a library is a library is a library. Without Camus or Sartre, for example, it's not a library."[9]

For the next few years, public librarians all over the country demonstrated their conviction that traditional library service was suitable and valuable for the disadvantaged. There was an explosion of outreach. The movement was strongly supported by radical and progressive librarians, those dedicated to populism and opposed to the war in Vietnam. The young activists arrived at the 1968 ALA conference in Kansas City determined to make the professional association an ally in their cause.

The tone of the 1968 conference was described in a *Library Journal* editorial: "A new urgency about social concerns, and the relevance of libraries and ALA to them; a swelling impatience with 'the establishment' and a demand for the involvement of youth; a veritable barrage of criticism . . . an insistent, rumbling awakening: That's what was happening in Kansas City."[10] The activist librarians called for the creation of an ALA Round Table on the Social Responsibilities of Libraries "to provide an outlet for expression of Libraries' and librarians' concerns on these issues—race, violence, war and peace, inequality of justice and opportunity."[11] The establishment agreed to consider the proposal.

The 1969 conference at Atlantic City was even more turbulent. The young activists, rumor had it, intended to disrupt the conference. Security measures quite foreign to librarians' meetings seemed necessary. In a noisy and confused gathering, the activists and the establishment quarreled over a resolution condemning the war in Vietnam. At other sessions, the activists presented a program for the reform of ALA. The establishment agreed to consider the program.

The movement to reform ALA was less than successful. The activists received encouraging words: "They have done a great service in disturbing our complacency," said ALA president William Dix in his 1969 inaugural address.[12] They won concessions: a Social Responsibilities Round Table and an office for service to the disadvantaged were established. But by January 1971, it was clear that ALA was resistant to reform. Nevertheless, the activist rebellion served notice on the public library community as a whole that times had changed.

Between 1967 and 1971, while the young activists were trying to reform ALA, the outreach movement ran its course. The spirit of outreach during those years was reflected in the opening paragraphs of a book entitled *Library Service to the Disadvantaged* published in 1971:

Psychedelic colors on storefront windows, karate and judo demonstrations, teen-agers swaying to a rock music concert, people playing checkers or chess in reading rooms . . . mothers drinking coffee, perhaps making clothes on donated sewing machines in a library room; children acting out a story; no fines for overdue books, no "hush-hush" signs anywhere in sight, wandering story tellers roaming the streets like Pied Pipers of Hamelin, leading groups of children to the friendly neighborhood library; gaily painted vehicles . . . stopping at street corners and showing films, playing records, and issuing books without the formality of a library card. . . . Can this be the American Public Library—that smug, impressive edifice that housed a multitude of books for the scholar, the researcher, the middle-class, average reader, lo these many years? It can be and it is. The new American public library has retraced its steps from a slow death march and has found a more proper role in society.[13]

The book described a host of outreach programs carried on around the country in both urban and rural areas. For the most part, the programs were traditional public library programs offered outside the library or offered to people who were traditionally numbered among the unserved. There were many story-telling programs for children: in the streets of poor neighborhoods; at day care centers, parks, playgrounds, community centers; housing projects, and bookmobile stops; and in schools for the children of migrant workers. Many outreach programs featured films, which were shown in vans and at various outdoor locations as well as at branch libraries in depressed neighborhoods. Many outreach programs placed book collections where they would be within easy reach: in housing projects, saloons, barbershops, community centers, private homes, churches, poolrooms, laundromats, and beauty shops. Some outreach programs used cars and vans to deliver books to busy intersections where sidewalk service was provided. Many programs involved bookmobiles. They went to inner-city schools, housing projects, block parties, Indian reservations, and migrant worker camps. Outreach during those years meant reaching out with traditional library services.

With the beginning of the new decade, the movement to bring traditional library services to the unserved collapsed. The High John library, a symbol of the movement, closed in September 1970. Two years later, an editorial in *Library Journal* reported that "you can count the number of outreach programs that have continued from those LBJ days on the fingers of one hand."[14] In the interval, the flurry of outreach ended.

Librarians had been told by those who knew that reaching out with traditional library services was a waste of time. By 1971, librarians agreed. They realized that the traditional public library cannot help the disadvantaged very much, that the library is a middle-class institution, alien and irrelevant in the ghetto, on the reservation, and in migrant worker camps. At a colloquium at the University of Maryland in 1973, a prominent black librarian, Milton Byam, director of the public library in Washington, D.C., said that every outreach program known to him was a failure.[15] Byam's experience was apparently general; and in the early years of the new decade, librarians who were advocates of service to the disadvantaged were seeking new forms of service that would allow the public library to play a more useful role in helping the disadvantaged, particularly the urban poor.

In October 1971, a conference at the University of Illinois explored what appeared to be a likely possibility. Conference planners stated:

The public library in the past few years has been looking for innovative approaches to inner-city service. Traditional library service is no longer adequate for serving the urban people. When librarians finally realized this they began searching for new approaches and ideas. Neighborhood information centers, envisioned as expanded reference services, are now beginning or under consideration in several urban libraries.[16]

A great deal of attention quickly turned to neighborhood information centers or community information centers as they came to be called. In February 1973, *Library Journal* reported that "news of community information activity is literally pouring into our offices from around the U.S."[17] The most publicized service offered by community centers and by central libraries as well became known as information and referral service (I & R). It was designed to enable clients to get in touch with agencies providing social services.

In the early 1970s, information and referral service seemed to have obvious value. It was the kind of service that would make the library useful in the inner-city and among the poor, would demonstrate the library's concern for the disadvantaged, and would appeal to funding authorities who wished to demonstrate their concern for the disadvantaged. Many libraries claimed to be offering I & R service. Not all of the claims were legitimate. In some cases, libraries pretending to offer I & R were simply providing "a reference service that has been part of their library operation at a low level for many years."[18] It was difficult to know what the phrase "information and referral" meant.

Thomas Childers, who did extensive investigations of public library I & R service in the middle and late 1970s, developed a definition. By Childers's definition, the service has four primary elements: (1) "simple information-giving"—providing "asked for information," (2) "complex information giving"—providing information "after probing to determine the inquirer's real underlying need," (3) "referral"—helping "the public make contact with an outside resource, by making an appointment, calling an agency, etc.," and (4) constructing a directory of services for the public to consult.[19]

Using that definition, Childers, as part of an extensive research project funded by the U.S. Office of Education, made inquires concerning the extent to which public libraries offer information and referral service. In 1978, he did a "focused survey" of 419 libraries that claimed to provide I & R or were "known" to provide it. He received 337 usable replies. Only 17 percent of the responding libraries offered referral as a "standard" service.[20] In 1979 and 1980, Childers made on-site investigations of seven libraries offering I & R. He found that "in all of the sites, I & R must be considered mostly 'I' and relatively little 'R.' The percentage of time the staff actually contact a resource on behalf of a client ('referral') ranges from 1 to 10%."[21]

In 1971, however, many librarians had hoped that information and referral service and community information centers would enable the professional community to plausibly claim that the public library was a people's institution.

It seemed imperative that the public library achieve or at least assume that identity. The failure of the outreach movement had conclusively demonstrated that the traditional public library is a middle-class institution. Folklore and public relations could no longer maintain otherwise. In 1971, the identification of the public library as a middle-class institution seemed a threat to its survival. Socially conscious, populist librarians were not interested in serving or in advocating service to the well-educated and relatively prosperous middle class; and they were not disposed to encourage or even allow their conservative colleagues to do so. Furthermore, conservative librarians and others who were merely opportunists realized that funding authorities were likely to be unmoved by pleas for money to support an institution that served the middle class. The populist social movement had done its work. Politicians had become populists. If the library could not become or at least appear to become a people's institution, it might indeed be on a slow death march.

Throughout the early 1970s, the public library community exhibited a sense of crisis. Wherever one looked, there seemed cause for alarm. There were economic problems: The bills for the Great Society and the Vietnam War were due; inflation was mounting; there was a recession in 1969–70. The older cities of the nation were decaying, suffering financial hardships that promised only to worsen. The libraries suffered with the cities. Middle-class library users were migrating to the suburbs. The old central libraries and many of their branches were surrounded by urban poor from whom the library could expect little support. And cities were not the only trouble spot. In relatively prosperous suburbs there was concern that the library would not be able to compete successfully for its share of the revenues paid by increasingly restive taxpayers.

There seemed to be other threats as well: increase in the costs of operation; the so-called knowledge explosion; the rise of the community college; the expansion and development of technology such as TV, cable, and especially computers. The whole array of circumstances and developments combined to create the librarian's nightmare: diminished revenues, increased costs, and the knowledge explosion together would progressively weaken library collections. The community college and the new media would decimate the library's clientele. Computers would bring forth wealthy and aggressive competitors who would make obsolete what was left of library service. The public library would die of starvation and neglect.

Early in 1971, the public library community roused itself to respond to the crisis. The Public Library Association began "a feasibility study in preparation for a major new inquiry into the goals of public libraries and their relevance to current social and economic factors."[22] The group responsible for the study did its work in record time. By March 1972, a report entitled *A Strategy for Public Library Change* was finished.

The introduction to the report referred to the crisis that prompted the study. "The fate ... of the public library is in question." Circulation is declining; "financial support ... is diminishing"; costs are rising; taxpayers are "rebellious"; competitors are "threatening to replace" the library. But if the right steps are taken, "a vital, purposeful agency will emerge" to "replace the passive, peripheral institution ... which has waited for people to seek its service." The introduction also described the study, which consisted of a survey of "pertinent" literature, interviews with "library leaders," and questionnaires sent to a sample of libraries and individuals. Included in the sample of libraries were those that participated in the Public Library Inquiry in the late 1940s.[23]

The document consisted of seven chapters. Chapter one described the "societal forces" that helped to create the crisis for public libraries such as social change, demographics, racial tension, and the knowledge explosion. Chapter two gave results of the questionnaire sent to the libraries that had participated in the Public Library Inquiry. The highlight was the disclosure that the libraries, with only one exception, rejected the recommendation of Berelson and Leigh that the public library concentrate on serving the minority of serious users. The respondents to the questionnaire "subscribe to 'service to all' as an article of faith."[24]

The third chapter, entitled "The Public Library Today," reported that the literature and the questionnaire responses were in substantial agreement concerning the "unique role of the public library." Everyone agreed that the library should provide "service to all," and resources for education, recreation, and cultural growth. Different respondents and sources used different terms and urged different priorities; but there was "general agreement" about what the library should be doing. "What then," the authors of the document asked, "is the problem?" The problem was that "statement and fulfillment are far apart."[25]

The reasons for the distance between statement and fulfillment were given in the next chapter, "Critical Problems." Twelve problems were presented— among them, finance and social change. The others concerned the library and librarians: poor public relations, librarians who were unwilling to change or lacked a "service orientation," "failure to serve all publics," poor library education, bad book selection, and a lack of cooperation among libraries. Yet other problems involved library management.[26]

The next chapter, entitled "Concensus on Goals," listed goals derived from responses to the questionnaire:

1) To provide service to all (stressed reaching unserved), 2) To provide information services, 3) To provide adult and continuing education, 4) To collect and disseminate all kinds of informational, educational and cultural materials, including non-print resources, 5) To support education—formal and informal, 6) To serve as a cultural center.[27]

The responses to the questionnaire that yielded the list of goals fell into two categories. The majority of respondents exhibited a "spirit of hope" that librarians "will become active agents serving the needs of society in positive, dynamic fashion." A minority of respondents exhibited a spirit of pessimism: the public library was "moving toward extinction."[28]

The final chapter made four recommendations: (1) "A publication should be commissioned which will be an eloquent statement to direct widespread attention to the American public library as an active community agent capable of meeting the real needs of real people." The publication should be accompanied by a documentary film. (2) An extensive program of research should be carried out. (3) The results of the research should be disseminated and demonstration libraries established. (4) Library education should be reformed. The recommendations did not call upon public libraries to do anything.[29]

A Strategy for Public Library Change was a hurried and confused response to the seeming crisis of the early 1970s. Librarians were deeply concerned that the public library would lose political and financial support if it did not change. Somehow, the library must become, or assume the appearance of, a people's institution. A tax-supported institution that lent books to a minority of well-educated, middle-class users seemed expendable. Librarians who honestly wished the library to be a people's institution and those who believed that it must be represented as such to funding authorities could speak with one voice.

But what were they to say? The old folklore, the trusty vehicle that delivered the Library Services Act and its sequels, was out of date. Everyone acknowledged that the traditional public library could not pass muster as a people's institution. Claims that the library could promote the intellectual and cultural advancement of the people with traditional services were futile after the recent failure of outreach. Furthermore, to suggest that the public library was necessary for the political enlightenment of the people went against the populist grain. Populism assumes that the people possess innate political wisdom.

A *Strategy for Public Library Change* proclaimed that "there is a clear mandate for a program of action which will enable the public library to fulfill its unique role in performing needed community functions which will be increasingly important in light of continuing changes in society."[30] But what kind of program of action and what needed functions were called for? The formal recommendations specified a public relations book, research, and education, a sign that the authors did not know what should be done. The document urged providing service to all and meeting the real needs of real people. How to serve all and what real needs to meet, the document left to others to discover.

A *Strategy for Public Library Change* was greeted with great enthusiasm. The president-elect of the Public Library Association said that it "marked the re-birth" of the organization and "infused" librarians "with new hope . . . new dedication."[31] Four "strategy groups" were appointed immediately to implement the document's four recommendations.

Implementation proved difficult. In December 1973, the *PLA Newsletter* announced that the recommended publication was to be a *Consumer's Handbook for Public Libraries*. The newsletter announced in March 1974 that funding for the publication was being sought (by October of that year funding had been obtained) and in March 1975 that authors had been recruited. In October 1975, the newsletter announced that publication was "eagerly anticipated" and that the publication would "be offered to publishers."[32] A search disclosed no further reference to the publication in the *PLA Newsletter*. Notices of the activities of the other strategy groups appeared in the newsletter for a while, then stopped.

Meanwhile, however, the project that A *Strategy for Public Library Change* failed to recommend formally but clearly envisioned was taken up by others. That project was to change the public library from a middle-class, peripheral institution into a "vital agency" that would provide "service to all" and "meet the real needs of real people." By the middle of 1973, a program to reform the public library was under way.

The people who launched the program had started out to perform a more limited task. Originally they were supposed to help the Public Library Association's Standards Committee decide what to do about national standards for public libraries. The standards of 1966 were obsolete when published. They were tied to the traditional public library. In 1972, they seemed more a cause of the current crisis than a tool for dealing with it. Yet no one knew how to go about replacing them. In January 1972, the final draft of *A Strategy for Public Library Change* was presented at a Public Library Association board meeting. The Standards Committee was present; and the document inspired the committee to act. With the help of three task forces, the Standards Committee took the first step in an effort "to determine effective new directions for the coordination and updating of existing public library standards."[33] The task forces were given one year to produce "working papers" for the "use and guidance" of the Standards Committee. The papers were supposed to "provide the committee with a conceptual framework within which to consider the philosophic implications of total community library service" on the development of standards.[34]

The working papers were published in the September 15, 1973, issue of *School Library Journal*. The most important one by the Task Force on Adult Services seemed to point out the way to make the public library the kind of institution envisioned in *A Strategy for Public Library Change*. The paper, its authors said, was "a philosophical statement on the future role of the public library . . . as an active, catalytic, and aggressive agency" meeting "certain expressed and unexpressed human needs" and "providing services for all people."[35]

In the opening paragraph, the authors identified a human need common to all people. "People need a variety of resources in order to flourish culturally, socially, physically, financially, politically and spiritually. . . . Among those resources is information."

The authors then provided a definition of information. They had forewarned their readers in the introduction that they would be using a "revised definition" of the term that must be "carefully read and understood" or the "significance" of the paper would be "missed." "Information," the authors stated, "includes not only facts and data, but also ideas and the products of man's creative endeavors." The definition named certain needs that are indeed common to all people, without which there would be no flourishing. Facts and ideas were indispensable. The authors finished the paragraph by saying that "the public library has been one of the institutions through which society has attempted . . . to provide each individual with equal and adequate access to informational resources." The authors seemed to suggest that the paper would reveal how the public library could take on a new role by meeting certain needs of all people for data, facts, and ideas, needs that must be met if people were to flourish.

In the next few paragraphs, the authors indicated what the library must do to meet its responsibility as an "information resource agency." The library "must ascertain and analyze" the community's information resources "in terms of the needs of the people." The library should "develop and maintain . . . a coordinated access system" so that "from whatever point an individual enters a community's configuration of resource agencies meeting human needs, that person will be efficiently directed to the appropriate service agency." The library "should serve as the core of a reliable information delivery system." The library should provide "active and reliable agents" who will "channel people to the sources that will meet their needs."

Succeeding paragraphs discussed more traditional matters. The library should provide "factual, educational, cultural and recreational materials"; "names and addresses of groups in the community or . . . of experts willing to share their skills"; materials of local interest; and cooperation with other community agencies. The paper concluded by recommending a strong public relations program and the recruitment and training of librarians who are "people-oriented."[36]

The working paper was brief; it took up slightly less than one page in the *School Library Journal*. The paper was very important, however, because it seemed to offer the solution to the problem—that of defining the new role of the public library as a people's institution. The old role had been repudiated; the old library was passive, peripheral, and middle-class. The new library was to be active, vitally important, and of service to all the people. The working paper, it seemed, provided the "philosophical" foundation for the transformation of the old library into the new.

The key seemed to be the new concept of information. Data, facts, and ideas were obviously essential to the flourishing condition of all people, as the paper indicated. The new role of the library would be to provide information in the sense of data, facts, and ideas. The paper briefly pointed out the way in which the library would perform its new role. The library would "ascertain and analyze" community information resources "in terms of the needs of the people" and help to meet those needs. The working paper thus seemed to break new theoretical ground with its new concept of information.

Actually, the paper did not break new ground and did not suggest a new role for the public library. It instead generated confusion about the role of the public library that spread throughout the professional community and led to years of wasted effort, to futile and expensive projects, and to the production of additional, even more confusing documents. By the end of the decade, the public library community seemed quite bewildered.

The principal defect of the working paper was its failure to make a critical distinction between two very different types of community information needs: the needs of the community for information in general and the needs of the community for information from the public library.

The working paper suggested that the public library could help in a significant way to meet community needs for information in general, needs for the data, facts, and ideas necessary for the community to flourish. The needs of a community for such information are virtually infinite in extent and complexity. No one has ever attempted to characterize or analyze the needs of a community for data, facts, and ideas or to ascertain how they might be met. Such a project is probably impossible. Those needs are beyond reckoning and the public library's role in meeting them is relatively insignificant.

The information needs that a public library can meet are those that can be met with library collections and a staff of librarians, needs that are limited, common to relatively few individuals and radically incommensurate with community needs for information in general. The working paper failed to note the library's limits and suggested that the library could meet community needs for information in general and that outrageous suggestion generated the confusion in the public library community.

The working paper of 1973 did its work. The public library community was captivated by the impression it conveyed that the library might provide important service to all. The professional community in 1973 was ready to accept almost anything that tendered that possibility. For almost twenty-five years, there had been no serious discussion of the purpose for the public library. A whole generation of librarians had grown up without ever being exposed to such a discussion, without ever seriously thinking about the matter. They were not well equipped to think about it in 1973. Some librarians did not seem to understand the concept of purpose and were prone to say, for example, that the purpose of the public library was to provide library service. The paper received no criticism. Librarians were reluctant to speak ill of documents written by colleagues. A silly paper by an important committee was likely to be praised or at least taken seriously. Also, there were librarians who cared little about how the library's purpose was presented so long as the presentation was good public relations. And finally, there were librarians who devoutly wished the library to be a people's institution and were ready to accept any document favorable to that wish. The public library community went to work to realize the working paper's vision of "the future role of the public library."

A document inspired by the working paper was presented to the PLA Standards Committee in January 1974. This document, like its predecessor, was supposed to help the Standards Committee solve the problem of national standards. The document was entitled "Design for Diversity." Early in the paper, the authors recommended that no new national standards be created. National standards were "rigid"; they were rules "for sameness"; they would not help librarians to "plan for the future." What librarians needed were "instruments" to help them understand their communities, "choose objectives in the light of that understanding," and measure success in attaining their objectives.[37]

The authors then provided a historical analysis of the traditional public library which they called "the prototype." After discussing its character and achievements, the authors concluded that the "prototype seems to be an anachronism." Therefore, it was necessary "to rethink the entire definition of public library goals."[38]

Next, the authors dealt with certain "difficulties," one being the meaning of the term information. The authors accepted the definition that their predecessors who wrote the working paper of 1973 "found that they had to create."

Information is data, facts, ideas, and so on. The authors of "Design for Diversity" seemed to sense that there might be some problems with that definition. They observed that sources of information include books, journals, films, and the like, but that sources also include "professional advisors . . . commercial agents, co-workers . . . family and friends." The authors did not attempt to address the problems raised by such an immensely general definition of information, one of which was the problem of distinguishing the sources that have to do with libraries from those that do not. The authors went on to deal with the next difficulty, the meaning of the term community. The authors identified and described two kinds: "place communities," such as towns, educational institutions, and businesses; and "interest communities," signifying groups interested in the same subject.

In their discussion of service to place communities, the authors emphasized the potential importance of the public library. It "is the most fundamental of the information agencies in a place" community. "Its primary purpose is to supply information to all people. . . . The public library should be the citizen's first resort when he has an information need." When specific services to a place community were mentioned, they recalled the prototype. The authors noted that the library could contribute to solving contemporary problems of crowding, noise, frustration, and alienation because it was a quiet, uncrowded place, provided materials for students so that "their school assignments do not become frustrating," and was a place to discover that "unorthodox" people "have been influential in society." The section on service to interest communities consisted mainly of a discussion of a hypothetical reference network that was the subject of an article in the *Bulletin of the Medical Library Association.*[39]

In the final section of the paper, the authors asked that the Standards Committee provide a set of "goals and guidelines" that could be used until new "tools" were devised that would enable librarians to "analyze a situation, set objectives, make decisions and evaluate achievements." The document closed with the statement that if society "decides to increase the amount of support given to public services, public libraries may well be entering a new era—one which will see them as a vitally important part of the life of every American community."[40]

Goals and guidelines were formulated without delay. They were given in a document entitled "Goals and Guidelines for Community Library Services," published in the June 1975 *PLA Newsletter*. The document was written by the Goals, Guidelines and Standards Committee, formerly the Standards Committee.

In the Introduction, the document acknowledged its forerunners: *A Strategy for Public Library Change*, the task force working paper, and "Design for Diversity." The next section, entitled Purpose, began as follows:

This statement of goals and guidelines describes the conceptual framework for a library service plan for the total community. . . . It is proposed that communities take a look at needs and resources, and develop a coordinated approach to total library and information services for every individual in the community.

The first goal, entitled Community Library Service, read as follows:

The American people need a variety of resources in order that they may flourish culturally, socially, physically, financially, politically and spiritually. The quality of life within the community is related to the excellence and availability of such resources. Among these resources is information, facts and data: and ideas and the products of man's creative endeavors. Library service to the total community is one of the means which society should use to insure the provision of informational resources.

Four guidelines followed the goal:

A. Library service is an active, catalytic and aggressive agency or array of agencies. B. Service is provided for all people.... C. Community information needs are ascertained and analyzed in order that a community's library service may respond fully to people's needs.... D. Communities have a system of library service that will provide coordinated access to the information resources in the community.

Five more goals followed, each with its own list of guidelines. The goals were entitled Freedom of Access, Management, Personnel, Materials, and Services and Programs.

The Freedom of Access goal called for "equal access to library materials, information and service existing in local, state and national systems" for "every individual member of a community." There were twelve guidelines under this goal. Total community library service was to be provided through cooperation between the public library and other types of libraries. Through cooperation "individuals are assured of access to knowledge of the world." So that needed materials and programs were provided, "all segments of the population" were to be consulted. Other guidelines provided in general terms for hours of service, location, space, and service to all age groups and groups with special needs.

The Management goal called for "informed, innovative, user oriented organization and administration." Nine guidelines provided for planning and other management responsibilities. "All agencies concerned with human needs" and "all segments of the population" were to be included in the planning process.

The Personnel goal called for "staffs ... capable ... of putting these goals and guidelines into effect." There were eight guidelines. The first stated that "staff are to be people-oriented. They should be knowledgeable, flexible, open, friendly, understanding, reliable, accessible, and active in the community." Other guidelines dealt briefly with training and the need to provide staff with opportunities for promotion and participation in management.

The Materials goal, the Services and Programs goal, and the guidelines listed under them called for a great variety of materials and services. Some of the guidelines provided for conventional materials and services that met needs for education, recreation, and so on. One guideline provided for information and referral service, another for programs and materials that would "foster a constructive attitude toward change" and be a "motivator and supplier of aspirations for the dispossessed and disorganized."[41]

"Goals and Guidelines for Community Library Services," the statement of an important PLA committee, gave official recognition and standing to the position taken in the task force working paper of 1973 and in "Design for Diversity": the public library could play an important role in meeting people's needs for information in general; the public library could and should ascertain, analyze, and respond to those needs.

"Goals and Guidelines for Community Library Services" was issued in June 1975 in response to a call for a temporary instrument for librarians to use until new tools could be fashioned. In October 1975, the president of PLA announced that the Goals, Guidelines and Standards Committee was going to "seek professional research assistance in order to develop new standards . . . based on 'Goals and Guidelines for Community Library Services'."[42]

But then early in 1976, the *PLA Newsletter* announced that the effort to create national standards had been abandoned. Instead of national standards, PLA would provide "a set of updated tools that will enable communities to plan and assess public library programs that will meet contemporary user needs."[43]

By spring 1976, PLA completed a research proposal that was the first step toward developing the new tools. The research proposal was entitled *The Process of Standards Development for Community Library Service*. The project was supposed to produce

tools, instruments, how-to-do-it manuals. . . . The intent is to enable a local community, library board or library manager to answer the following questions: 1) What are the library/information needs of this community? 2) What is adequate library service for this community? 3) What is the expected cost . . . ? 4) What part shall this public library, as one institution in the local array, play in meeting the community's needs?[44]

Finally work was to begin that would furnish the practical instruments that would enable the library to assume its new role in society. In August 1977, the U S Office of Education provided $140,000 to fund the project; and a company known as King Research, Inc., went to work on it.

Since the projects to produce the new tools and manuals would take a long time, the PLA Board asked the Goals, Guidelines and Standards Committee to "prepare an interim document to guide public library managers and lay decision makers in their efforts to see that their communities receive the level of library services they need and deserve."[45] A document written in response to that request was approved by the PLA Board and published in the December 1977 issue of *American Libraries*. Entitled "A Mission Statement for Public Libraries," it began by observing that "the nation's public libraries are in serious trouble." They were "geared" to the needs of nineteenth-century society. The present needs of society "demand that the public library . . . assume a strong leadership role." The document then described some of the "factors in American society demanding a new institution." One was "runaway social change." Because of that threat, "society needs an agency to operate, as it were, in the eye of the revolutionary storm, to keep the radical new thrust in some continuity with the past." A second factor was the "exponential increase in the volume and complexity of the record of human experience." Because of this, "society needs an agency to guide the user . . . to . . . materials to meet each individual's need for information, knowledge and ideas." The third factor was "total egalitarianism." Because everyone is equal, "society needs an agency that can actively bring every person, regardless of age, education, language, religion, ethnic and cultural background, and mental and physical health, into effective contact with the human record." The fourth factor was "depletion of natural resources." Because of this, "society needs an agency to help people keep abreast of the ecological facts . . . to separate ecological truth from . . . propaganda."

The document then paused "before examining responses to today's societal needs" in order to "look at several key words"—words that "once described adequately the traditional function of the public library" but no longer did so. The document provided a glossary. "*Access* now implies innovative, imaginative delivery techniques which overcome geographic, educational, physical and psychological barriers." *Community* meant the entire world and "literally everyone." The term "*information* now includes not only the sum total of recorded human experience—factual, imaginative, scientific and humanistic—but also the unrecorded experience . . . to which library users may be referred." The last term was *target groups* which meant "all current and potential individuals and groups in society." Other terms in the glossary such as *selection* and *management* did not lend themselves to cosmic definitions.[46]

The document concluded by listing the specification for an "information agency" capable of responding to the "social needs of today." Such an agency would need to be part of a worldwide network. It would need to collect, organize, and translate "the human record on all intellectual levels." It would have to dramatize the importance of the human record and help to decide which portion of that record to "erase." Finally, such an agency would need to present the human record to those who had been kept from it because of "lack of education, lack of language facility, ethnic or cultural backgrounds, age, physical or mental handicaps and apathy." The document recognized that public libraries alone could not meet all of the specifications. All libraries must help. The public library, however, would play an important part, "leading all libraries in their response to today's new social needs."[47]

The document thus continued the series that began with the working paper of 1973. The "Mission Statement" presented the library's future role in more grandiose terms than its predecessors; and like its predecessors, it did not say how the library was to carry out such a wonderful mission. But that task was not being neglected. The research project that was to develop "tools, instruments, how-to-do-it manuals" was in progress.

The issue of *American Libraries* that published the "Mission Statement" also published some reactions to it. The commentators took the document seriously, calling it "dramatic," "controversial," "helpful," and "very welcome."[48] Six years after the "Mission Statement" was published, when no one any longer cared about it, an individual who was "part of the committee who wrote the thing," appraised the document by calling it "one of the most awful collections of contradictory, sanctimonious gibberish ever assembled in an attempt to keep everyone happy. . . . We tried to throw everyone a bone, perpetuating the idea that public libraries should serve everyone, fulfill all our social responsibilities, guarantee all librarians jobs they liked, assure the rights of minorities, and bring plentiful water to the desert of Arizona."[49]

But the worst was yet to come. The president's program at the 1978 midwinter meeting of ALA featured a discussion of a paper written by a committee of seven librarians appointed by the president of ALA. The paper, entitled "Toward a Conceptual Foundation for a National Information Policy," was "a statement aimed at stirring discussion throughout the library community."[50] The authors were public librarians, library school professors, or staff members at library systems or state libraries. The paper opened with reflections on the importance of information. People need information in order to "enhance the quality" of their participation "in the decisions of the nation." People need information in order to "live productive lives in physical, mental and moral strength, and to pursue the intellectual and spiritual fulfillment of their myriad and diverse motivations." Information is "a vital fluid coursing throughout the body politic essential to its continuing renewal and growth."

Because information is so important, American society must "reaffirm its mandate to its publicly-supported libraries to seek out and deliver to all people the information they need or desire. . . . *All information* must be available to *all people* in *all formats* purveyed through *all communication channels* and delivered at *all levels of comprehension*. . . . All information means *all* information. . . . Everyone means everyone." If anything less is done, "the whole is enervated, and the national enterprise as a consequence suffers."[51]

After explicating the "universals" quoted above, the document closed by giving notice that the cost of delivering all information to everyone was high and must be borne by all levels of government. The document was the last in the series proclaiming a new role for the public library. It was the ultimate statement. It was impossible to imagine a more stupendous role for the public library. All information for everyone was the absolute limit.

During the years when the documents analyzed above were being written, many libraries were making independent efforts to assume the identity of a people's institution. These libraries were not ascertaining and meeting information needs. They were offering programs and services that they hoped would attract a lot of people to the library. While official documents magnified the importance of the library's contribution to society, the trend in the field was to trivialize the library. It was a sympton of the confusion of the time. As the official documents reached higher altitudes, the library's purpose became more and more unclear.

The list of new programs and services intended to popularize the library was long. Some of the items were strange; and some were very strange. A library in Minnesota played video tapes of the Vikings's games twice on Wednesdays for football fans who had missed the games on the weekends. A library in Phoenix sold garbage bags at the request of city officials. A library in a depressed neighborhood distributed rat poison. Libraries in many neighborhoods distributed tax forms and registered voters. Around the country, libraries provided programs or demonstrations of many kinds: sky diving, beer can collecting, coupon or comic book swapping, mountain climbing, belly dancing, skateboarding, lock picking, hair styling, safe cracking, and bicycle repair. Libraries held business breakfasts, exercise sessions, and grafitti contests. Libraries lent jewelry, sculpture, plants, smoke alarms, art prints, cameras, and tools. Librarians who could not make head or tail of their profession's official documents explained such antics by vacuous talk of serving the people. One expected that librarians would soon be shining shoes and washing cars.

In 1979, a report in *Publishers' Weekly* caused a sensation in the public library community by describing what was going on at the Baltimore County Public Library. The library was placing branches, called minilibraries, in shopping malls. The minilibraries were like retail outlets for popular books except that the minilibraries passed out books free of charge: "Filled with bright, illuminated fixtures, dumps heavy with the latest romances, shelves stacked with best sellers and paperbacks, this library has no card catalogue, reference section or study areas—nothing to hint that it is anything other than a typical bookstore in a desirable, high traffic location." The theory behind the minilibraries was stated by the chief of the Baltimore County Library, Charles Robinson: "The public pays for the library, so the public should get what it wants." To implement the theory, best sellers were bought in huge numbers. The library anticipated demand "by keeping up with advertising budgets, media events and hype." Books that did not circulate were weeded. One branch sold poetry books to make room on the shelves

for "romances, gothics, mysteries and media tie-ins." The article in *Publishers'*
Weekly made Baltimore County sound like the trash capital of the world.[52]

The theory and practice of the Baltimore County Public Library attracted
a great deal of attention. Robinson and his lieutenants were much in demand
at meetings and conferences. The theory appeared to be populist—the people
should be given what they want. The practice appeared to be successful—
Baltimore County Public Library had the highest per capita circulation in
the country.

Other new developments reported during the years 1973–79 were reminiscent of the traditional public library but had a populist flavor. Many
libraries reported programs or projects in oral history or local culture.

None of the new programs and services reported during those years meas-
ured up to the new role that the documents of the professional community
envisioned for the public library, a vital role in helping to meet the information needs of society. Ever since 1972, when *A Strategy for Public Library*
Change proclaimed the need for a new public library, the professional community had been waiting for some kind of blueprint for the new institution.
Since 1976, a research team had been at work on a project that would help
to bring the library of the future into existence. In the spring of 1980, the
long-awaited document, *A Planning Process for Public Libraries*, was published.

In January 1978, the research team leader had clarified what the project
intended to accomplish. The project would produce "a planning process
which any public library (system) can use to plan and evaluate service programs that are appropriate to the needs of its specific community." The
planning process would consist of three steps. First, the planners would
"determine community information needs and resources." Second, the planners would evaluate community information resources. Third, the planners
would establish goals, objectives and, priorities.[53] The third step would be
based on the first two.

The first step of the planning process, the team leader said, would enable
planners to "determine community information needs and resources." Apparently that meant needs for data, facts and, ideas and community resources
for meeting those needs. Subsequent planning steps would depend on the
extent of needs and resources discovered during the first step.

But the notion that library planners or anyone else could determine such
needs or resources was astounding. One could hardly imagine library planners questioning the people about their needs for data, facts, and ideas or
what people would make of such a question. Nor could one imagine any
source that planners might consult to discover, for example, what facts and
ideas were needed by the people of Minneapolis in 1980. People needed these
resources, but the extent of that need was unknowable. It was extremely
doubtful that anything sensible could be said about one person's needs, much
less a whole community's.

It was also impossible to determine a community's information resources, its inventory of data, facts, and ideas. Presumably this would involve adding up all the data on record in the community, plus all the facts people know, plus all the ideas in their heads and elsewhere. The notion of such an inventory being possible was outlandish.

At the same time, however, it seemed that in 1978 the research team leader promised a planning process that would enable library planners to determine community information needs and resources. Public library documents had repeatedly defined information as data, facts, and ideas. If the planning process did not show how to determine needs for data, facts, and ideas and the extent to which the community already possessed data, facts, and ideas would not the professional community be disappointed? And if the planning process did not show planners how to determine the aforementioned needs and resources, would it show them how to do something else? If so, what would that be; and how would the public library community react?

The answers to those questions became available when *A Planning Process* was published in 1980. The document did not give prescriptions for determining community information needs and resources, because those things could not be done. What the document gave instead was a set of planning prescriptions so obscure and confused that the public library community could not really figure out what the document provided. But the professional community's idea of what it wanted was also obscure and confused; librarians therefore did not know whether the document provided what they wanted or not. For a while, they accepted the document as a guide to planning the library of the future. Use of the document was widely advocated. Innumerable meetings were held to discuss it. Many libraries tried to create planning projects in accordance with its prescriptions. Then, after a few years, the uselessness of the document became obvious; and the public library community simply abandoned it, without saying why, perhaps without knowing why. *A Planning Process*, as well as the public library community's reception of it and efforts to use it, added up to a complete fiasco.

A Planning Process was an impressive-looking, 304-page document. But most of it was introduction and appendixes. The planning process itself was presented in Part II of the document, entitled "The Planning Process." The first chapter of Part II was supposed to deal with the first step, determining the information needs of the community.

The effort began bravely with a definition of purpose: "The ultimate purpose of any library," the authors said, "is to meet the information needs of its community." The authors then defined information. "The term information, as used here, includes all knowledge, ideas, facts, and imaginative works of the mind which have been communicated, recorded, published and/ or distributed formally or informally in any format."[54] But there was no way in the world that the authors could even begin to discuss community needs for all knowledge, ideas, and facts; so immediately, without explaining or calling attention to what they were doing, the authors restricted the scope of their concern to types of information that public libraries had always provided. The authors were concerned only with what they called "background," "subject," and "coping" information. This was a drastic restriction of scope; but the authors really had no choice. They could not possibly have dealt with community needs for all knowledge, ideas and, facts.

The authors then provided definitions of the types of information with which they would be concerned. Background information was that which "provides an understanding of self and others, of . . . historical and cultural roots . . . the elements of knowledge. . . . The library provides . . . background information through its collection of print and non-print materials (fiction and non-fiction), and through its programming and reference services. A substantial amount of this information is provided by leisure or recreational reading—reading for pleasure." Subject information referred to a "subject area which is related to interests or activities." It was provided to students, professionals, farmers, and so on. Coping information was that which was "needed to make decisions and solve problems. . . . Coping questions tend to be referred to the library in relatively few cases."[55] Coping information looked very much like information provided by traditional reference service and information and referral service.

Having identified and defined the three types of information, the authors concluded the chapter by offering suggestions for determining the extent of community needs for background, subject, and coping information. What the authors proposed would do no more than reveal the extent of needs for traditional library service.

In the next chapter, entitled "Current Library Services and Resources," the authors provided prescriptions for evaluating the library's ability to meet community information needs. The authors prescribed analysis of library materials, staff, programs, and facilities. Investigations of reference and circulation statistics were recommended. "Adequacy of performance" was indicated by "the proportion of community residents using the library." The appraisal of the library that was prescribed would reveal the extent to which the library was effective in providing traditional library service.[56]

Nowhere did the authors make any attempt to give suggestions for determining "community information resources" in the sense of data, facts, and ideas, as the team leader once indicated the project would do. The team had undoubtedly discovered the impossibility of doing so.

By the end of the chapter on appraising library resources and services, the authors had given directions for determining community needs for background, subject, and coping information and for appraising the library's ability to meet those needs. The question at this point was, what would be authors do next? The next logical step seemed to be suggesting a set of planning prescriptions for making improvements in the library so that it would be more effective in meeting community needs in the three areas specified. Such suggestions might include tips for identifying and establishing priorities, setting goals and objectives, and devising a plan of action.

But if the authors proceeded that way, it would be apparent that they were prescribing a planning process for the traditional library—the old peripheral prototype anachronism that had been providing background, subject, and coping information to a minority of middle-class users for more than a hundred years. Such a planning process was definitely not what they were expected to provide and not what they had promised.

In the third chapter of Part II, the authors escaped from their predicament by introducing a planning step that had nothing to do with the previous two stages. This chapter called for planners to determine "the role of the library in the community." The authors identified this as the key planning step. "The definition of role is critical to the planning process, since it forms the basis for everything that comes later. . . . The goals and objectives which detail exactly what the library plans to do stem from it."[57] The authors thus indicated that the process begun in earlier chapters was finished and would play no further part in planning.

The authors then gave a mystifying idea of what a role statement should look like. "It is not a broad mission statement so much as an action statement that describes in global terms what the library is going to do . . . to serve the needs of its community."[58] What could one make of that? Other general hints for formulating a role statement were confusing and not at all helpful. The kind of statement the authors envisioned at this most important stage of the planning process was a complete puzzle.

Then the authors came to the rescue. They provided four examples of role statements. The examples made it clear what the authors had in mind. The examples were all very similar. None included any reference to background, subject, or coping information. The following example is representative:

[The library] will supply promptly the most-wanted materials and services for adults and juveniles; will develop and implement appropriate services for the aging; will coordinate and host special learning programs for the illiterate, and develop non-print and print collections relevant to their needs and the needs of new literates. [The library will] provide convenient hours and points of access and appropriate library services for all community residents.[59]

In all four examples, part of the library's role was to provide most-wanted materials. That came as a bit of a surprise. Otherwise, all the examples described the library's role in terms that were very general and quite obvious. The role statement quoted above said that the library would provide "appropriate library services," "relevant" collections, "convenient hours and points of access." Other examples said that the library would provide "needed special services," "any needed information," and "rapid access"; and that the library would "not unnecessarily duplicate" the services of other libraries.

Two of the examples said that the library would provide "appropriate" or "special" services for "the aging." Most public libraries had no alternative but to attempt all of those things. Library officials who needed to go through a planning process to discover such roles would be a very dull-witted group indeed. Apart from the references to providing most-wanted materials, almost any public library in the country could formulate a role statement faithful to the examples without spending five minutes on a planning process.

On the other hand, the appearance of the phrase "most-wanted" in all the model role statements was a surprise. Nothing in the document had prepared the reader for that phrase in such a key context. There was not a word anywhere in the chapter on role definition to explain why providing most-wanted materials should be part of any public library's role, much less part of the role of public libraries in general as was suggested by the frequent appearance of the phrase. Yet, suggesting by repetition that libraries should, in the future, provide most-wanted materials did create certain impressions. First of all, the repeated phrase suggested that the planning process was for the library of the future, not the traditional library. In 1980, asserting that the library should, above all, meet popular demand was considered radical and innovative. A planning document that highlighted the importance of providing most-wanted materials would hardly be mistaken as a guide to planning traditional service. In addition, the emphasis on providing most-wanted materials gave A *Planning Process* the desired populist flavor. A planning document so friendly to public demand seemed to be a planning document for a people's library.

With the chapter on role definition, the document fell apart. Role definition was presented as the key step; but it had no connection with the planning process begun in earlier chapters. General directions for formulating a role statement were vague and confused. Tendentious examples of role statements were given. In part, the examples proposed roles for the library so obvious that no planning effort was needed to identify or select them. Otherwise, the examples arbitrarily suggested that the role of the public library in general was to provide materials in response to public demand. The document, in its critical section, Part II, was so defective that it could not be used to guide a serious and intelligent planning effort.

The public library community, confused for years by other perplexing documents, accepted A *Planning Process*. It was big and impressive. Its confusion seemed to facilitate its acceptance in that no one could be sure it did not provide what was wanted. It seemed to have the desired flavor—nontraditional and populist. The document was well received in the spring of 1980. During the next three or four years, eons were wasted by innumerable groups across the country as they gathered to discuss the document. A few trifling defects were discovered; but the major flaws never surfaced in the discussion. Many libraries tried to use the document for planning. The planning efforts produced role statements that were faithful to the models in *A Planning Process*—that is, general and obvious. A library system in an eastern state that claimed to have used the document for planning produced the following role statement: "The _____County Library System exists for the purpose of providing quality library services to the citizens of _____ County. It will perform this mission by stimulating and assisting the member libraries to provide effective services and providing library services directly when deemed appropriate."[60] One wonders how much time it took to discover such a role.

The publication of *A Planning Process* was supposed to inaugurate the era of the public library as a vital institution serving all. The document did not do that. But by the time the document appeared and made the rounds of discussions and attempts to use it, the temper of the public library community had changed. The sense of crisis that led to the document's creation had faded. Constant and urgent calls for a new public library were no longer heard.

A Strategy for Public Library Change, the first proclamation of crisis, was published in 1972. Ten years is a long time to keep a sense of crisis alive; a crisis lasting so long tends to lose its credentials. By 1981 and 1982, some librarians were tired of hearing about the crisis, tired of hearing about meeting the information needs of society. Some had the good sense to be put off by the extravagance of the documents of the late 1970s. Some simply despaired of the public library's ability to become something other than what it had been. In addition, economic circumstances contributed to the closing of the crisis period.

The late 1970s and early 1980s were years of economic disaster. The price of oil made serious inflation worse. The early years of the Reagan presidency were years of virtual depression. Economic hardship and growing revulsion against public spending made the public library community in general despair of increased funding. Even if librarians could figure out how to create the library of the future, that library, it appeared, would be no more prosperous than the library of the past. The vision of the library as the provider of information for the people faded in the early 1980s.

NOTES

1. Godfrey Hodgson, *America in Our Time* (Garden City, N.Y.: Doubleday, 1976), 307.

2. Charles A. Reich, *The Greening of America* (New York: Random House, 1970), 4.

3. Foster E. Mohrhardt, "Libraries Unlimited," *ALA Bulletin* 61 (July-August 1967): 811.

4. Edwin Castagna, "A Troubled Mixture," in *Conference on Library Service to the Unserved, University of Wisconsin—Milwaukee, November 16–18, 1967* (New York: Bowker, 1970), 15.

5. Richard Moses, "The Training of Librarians to Serve the Unserved," in *Conference on Library Service to the Unserved*, 74.

6. Eva G. Williams, "Personnel and Materials for the Unserved," in *Conference on Library Service to the Unserved*, 84.

7. Jimmii Givings, "How the Urban Community Copes with the Central Core as Seen by the Residents, Part 2," in *Conference on Library Service to the Unserved*, 35.

8. News, *Library Journal* 92 (August 1967): 2702.

9. Eric Moon, "High John," *Library Journal* 93 (January 15, 1968): 150.

10. Editorial, *Library Journal* 93 (August 1968): 2775.

11. Kenneth Duhac, "A Plea for Social Responsibility," *Library Journal* 93 (August 1968): 2799.

12. "The New Constituency," *Library Journal* 94 (August 1969): 2738.

13. Eleanor Frances Brown, *Library Service to the Disadvantaged* (Metuchen, N.J.: Scarecrow, 1971), 1.

14. Editorial, *Library Journal* 97 (October 1, 1972): 3101.

15. John C. Colson, "The Agony of Outreach," *Library Journal* 98 (October 1, 1973): 2817. See also Richard Moses, "Hindsight on High John," *Library Journal* 97 (May 1, 1972): 1672–74.

16. Carol L. Cronus and Linda Crowe, "Rationale for a Conference," in *Libraries and Neighborhood Information Centers* (Urbana: University of Illinois Graduate School of Library Science, 1972), viii.

17. Editorial, *Library Journal* 98 (February 15, 1973): 487.

18. Thomas Childers, *Information and Referral: Public Libraries* (Norwood, N.J.: Ablex, c1984), 19.

19. Ibid., 16.

20. Ibid., 12–14, 26.

21. Ibid., 212.

22. News, *Library Journal* 96 (September 15, 1971): 2715.

23. Allie Beth Martin, *A Strategy for Public Library Change* (Chicago: ALA, 1972), vii, ix.

24. Ibid., 18.

25. Ibid., 20–22.

26. Ibid., 26–45.

27. Ibid., 46.

28. Ibid., 46, 48.

29. Ibid., 50–52.

30. Ibid., 50.

31. *PLA Newsletter* 12 (March 1973): 1, 3–4.

32. *PLA Newsletter* 14 (October 1975): 1.

33. *PLA Newsletter* 11 (October 1972): 1.

34. "Community Library Services—Working Papers on Goals and Guidelines," *School Library Journal* (September 15, 1973): 21–22.

35. Ibid., 23.

36. Ibid., 23–24.

37. Ralph Blasingame and Mary Jo Lynch, "Design for Diversity," *PLA Newsletter* 13 (June 1974): 5–6.

38. Ibid., 10–11.

39. Ibid., 11–18.

40. Ibid., 19–20.

41. "Goals and Guidelines for Community Library Services," *PLA Newsletter* 14 (June 1975): 10–12.

42. *PLA Newsletter* 14 (October 1975): 3.

43. *PLA Newsletter* 15 (Winter/Spring 1976): 3.

44. *The Process of Standards Development for Community Library Service* (Chicago: Public Library Association, 1976), 4.

45. "A Mission Statement for Public Libraries," *American Libraries* 8 (December 1977): 616.

46. Ibid., 616–18.

47. Ibid., 618–20.

48. Ibid., 618–19.

49. Charles W. Robinson, "Libraries and the Community," *Public Libraries* 22 (Spring 1983): 10.

50. "Four New 'Takes' on 1978 Activity from the ALA Midwinter Meeting," *American Libraries* 9 (March 1978): 132.

51. *Toward a Conceptual Foundation for a National Information Policy* (Chicago: American Library Association, 1978), 1–2.

52. Kenneth C. Davis, "The Selling of the Library," *Publishers' Weekly* (August 13, 1979): 26–28.

53. Vernon Palmour and Marcia Bellassai, "Towards Public Library Standards," *Public Libraries* 17 (Summer 1978): 4–5.

54. Vernon E. Palmour, Marcia C. Bellassai, and Nancy V. DeWath, *A Planning Process for Public Libraries* (Chicago: American Library Association, 1980), 41.

55. Ibid., 41–45.

56. Ibid., 47–51.

57. Ibid., 52.

58. Ibid.

59. Ibid., 56.

60. "More News of Public Libraries Planning," *Public Libraries* 21 (Summer 1982): 62.

8

A Step in the Right Direction

1980–1987

By the early 1980s, the movement to create the public library of the future had run its course. The question was, what would happen next? It seemed unlikely that the public library community would concoct some grand new scheme for providing service to all. The schemes of the past decade had failed. Librarians were likely to regard similar new ventures with skepticism.

The flurry of planning instigated by *A Planning Process* would provide no new direction. The document encouraged aimlessness. There seemed a possibility that the professional community might spend the decade making plans to provide "appropriate services," "needed information," and "most-wanted" materials.

Some other signs were not encouraging. In 1982, ALA published a document entitled *Output Measures for Public Libraries* that offered twelve statistical measures for determining library "output." *Output Measures* was greeted with jubilation. Librarians were delighted to have a set of measures that would enable colleagues all over the country to count outputs in a uniform way. *Output Measures*, it seemed, might lead to an unprecedented statistical frenzy. And librarians would spend the decade counting outputs.

The document itself gave no offense. The measures it recommended seemed sensible enough. The danger was that the measuring exercises the document made possible combined with the current fixation on outputs would lead to the compilation of mountains of meaningless statistics, an enormous waste of time and effort.

Library statistics are valuable only to the extent that they indicate the library's success in fulfilling its purpose. Neither measuring outputs nor increasing them constitutes a purpose. If librarians are confused about purpose or define the library's purpose in meaningless terms such as providing appropriate services, then counting outputs is a worthless exercise.

In addition, excessive concern for statistics may have a darker side.

Librarians have never given enough attention to the possibility that statistics may be used primarily to advance the private and personal purposes of librarians. Librarians may work to increase statistics of circulation, program attendance, and registration primarily to advance their careers and reputations and to secure or increase their incomes. When that happens, the library is placed in the personal service of those who manage it; and that is dishonest and corrupt. Concern for statistics in the absence of concern for purpose may indicate merely lack of seriousness and intelligence; but it may also indicate corruption. When librarians are unconcerned about purpose or satisfied with unclear, overblown, and unrealistic definitions of purpose (or with no definition at all) and, at the same time, are deeply concerned about statistics, then suspicion is justified. In the early 1980s, enthusiasm about *Output Measures* was not matched by any great concern for identifying or clarifying the library's purpose.

Another discouraging sign appeared in the late 1970s and was still very much in evidence in the mid–1980s, namely, a campaign urging librarians to engage in "marketing" the library. In 1984, a book promoting the idea said that marketing "is the 'in' word of the year in Libraryland."[1]

Advocates portrayed marketing as an "exchange relationship." The community provided money and library users. "In exchange, the library must return to the community the best possible response to their [sic] needs." What needs the library must respond to were not clear and did not appear to be a matter of intense concern. The main concern of marketing advocates was increasing library use. But promoting use of the library for education is not the stuff of good marketing. Librarians who practice "ineffective marketing" believe that "a public library should be dedicated to the continuing education of the common man." Librarians who practice "effective marketing" believe that "the functions of recreational reading and information services in a public library are ends in themselves."[2]

A 1979 editorial in *Library Journal* identified marketing as a "current fad." Marketing "sounds suspiciously like a host of activities in which librarians have engaged for years, under such disguises as public relations, circulation, publicity, shelving and community analysis."[3] Marketing in the mid–1980s was no more than public relations with a new name, another futile effort to make the library attractive to nonusers. Marketing seems to have been inspired by excessive concern for statistics; suspicion of corruption was justified.

While *Output Measures* and marketing were the center of attention, however, there were also signs of intelligence and vitality in the public library community. In 1977, a reference librarian at an Oklahoma City library published an article entitled "A Critique of the Progressive Public Library Movement in America." The progressive movement to which the title referred was the one, then in full career, to create the public library of the future, serving all and meeting distinctive community needs. The author, Judith McPheron, had doubts about the "community" progressive librarians talk about. In reality, McPheron said, American "communities" were, to a deplorable extent, local centers of "mass culture" marked by "conformity and sameness" propagated by "the manipulative powers and huge growth of the advertising industry and communications network." Progressive librarians, intentionally or not, were working to make a bad situation worse. "Responsiveness to community desires means responsiveness to advertising overkill." Much damage had already been done. "In our responsiveness to community, our shelves are filled, overwhelmingly, with pulp fiction, and how-to books. . . . Public libraries, especially branch libraries, are numbling in their regularity. Take out local histories and geneological materials, and we are the suburbanization of the mind." What the library ought to provide were materials that offered "a basis for serious thought and ideas." McPheron acknowledged that "people, especially poor people, have more immediate needs" and that it was true to some extent that the ability to "read serious material" was not general in the population. Yet development was possible. To abandon the effort to promote that development

even when it seems most difficult, is not to cheer for democracy and equality. . . . If democracy is defined as reducing human capabilities to the degree that we are all zombies, and therefore equal, then it is not worth having. If, instead, it is defined as the shared encouragement and development of the best of human potential, equally and for all, then it is not only worth having, but the one thing worth having. . . . But libraries, especially public libraries, have a chance to foster that kind of social growth only if they collect, organize, and make accessible those materials which stimulate and encourage serious thought.[4]

McPheron's article received no widespread acclaim or official notice, which was not surprising. It was published at a time when the progressive movement was still soaring. McPheron did, however, receive quiet but suitable recognition. Her article was selected for republication by those responsible for a collection entitled *The Best of Library Lit. 1977.*

Five years later, in 1982, when the progressive movement was defunct and the public library community was beginning to appreciate the futility of *A Planning Process*, there were three notable attempts to guide the public library toward a better course. Thomas Ballard, librarian of the Plainfield, New Jersey, Public Library, in an article in the *Public Library Quarterly*, reminded librarians that the public library was essentially an educational institution. The tax paying public, Ballard stated, "supports the library as an educational agency in the community." Librarians, therefore, were obliged to operate the library as such an agency. In responding primarily to the demands of library users who want recreation, librarians were ignoring the wishes of most taxpayers who believe that "recreational services are best financed by those using them. . . . Many of the activities on which public librarians pride themselves have a tenuous relationship to education at best. This must stop."[5]

The September 15, 1982, issue of *Library Journal* published an article by Murray C. Bob, director of a library system in Jamestown, New York. Bob's article also attacked the position that the library should seek primarily to satisfy the demands of library users. Bob's position was that "public libraries are publicly supported to serve as agencies of informal, self-motivated, self-regulated self-education." Tax money "is certainly not primarily given to libraries in order that they act as purveyors of perishable and popular items of interest and use to only a small segment of the population, for a couple of weeks or months—no matter how much circulation is achieved. Indeed, if public authorities pay any attention whatever to circulation, it is because librarians foolishly keep talking of only that." Bob's view of the library's obligation to society was similar to McPheron's. "Libraries have a responsibility to ideas, to nurturing, sustaining, preserving, and making readily available the intellectual capital of our society to anyone who may want or need it, now or in the future. Collections are built to serve over time. By doing that we show responsibility to the citizens who pay for the service."[6]

But the most important and influential of the voices raised in 1982 was that of Lowell Martin. In the 1982 Bowker Memorial Lecture, Martin, then a venerable figure in the library establishment, made a plea to public librarians to restore the failing vitality of the public library. In his address, Martin viewed the public library as if it were a middle-aged person faced with a crisis. One course of action chosen by such a person would lead to years of vigor and productivity, another course to decline ending in death. If the library did not choose the right course, it would "slip into premature old age."[7]

Martin, characteristically, diagnosed the library's ills in a way that would not give offense to colleagues. He did not say that the library suffered from the confusion, pretentiousness, insecurity, and self-regard of many in the profession. He said rather that the library suffered from having attempted too much, from an "overload of good works." The library had tried to be "the people's university, the student's auxiliary, the children's door to reading, the free bookstore, the information agency, the scholar's workshop and the community center." But there was a "fatal gap between claims and accomplishments, between expectation and reality, between aspiration and resources."[8]

Martin gave a prescription: The library must stop trying to do all the things it had been doing. It must select from among the roles it had played and tried to play. The library must "concentrate and strengthen."[9]

Martin considered the various roles the library had played in its effort to do too much. He expressed doubts about several. Performing as the scholar's workshop was beyond the capability of all but the largest libraries. Performing as the student's auxiliary involved a certain difficulty. Students tended to want what libraries, as a matter of policy, did not buy. Making the library an effective community center called for fundamental changes that "few libraries are prepared to contemplate." Martin also had doubts about the role of the library as a free bookstore. This "role for a publicly-supported agency will be challenged." It might be "the easy way out in the short term"; but "in the long run" such a role would be questioned by "hard-pressed municipal authorities." Children's service, Martin said, was "deservedly entrenched" in the public library as a "bright jewel." But, he said, use of the library by children was declining. Martin hoped that something can be done about this.[10]

The other two roles Martin mentioned were the information center and the people's university. Concerning the first, he said that the public library might find its place in "the information complex"; but he doubted that the library could be *the* information center." There was too much information; and there were too many sources. Nevertheless the library could perhaps find a role providing information to help satisfy "that range of curiousity, and aspiration and appreciation" characteristic of "the alert, sensitive, adventurous human being."[11]

Martin then characterized the role of the people's university as "the older concept" of the library as a "cultural-educational-recreational resource."[12] Martin's discussion of this role, which he clearly favored, recalled Leigh's discussion of the library's "natural role" in the final report of the Public Library Inquiry in 1950. "Given," Martin said, "the communication matrix" of today's society with its flood of information and print, would we, if there were no public library, "now press for its establishment? If so, for what purpose?":

One answer is that people, at least some part of the populace, want a place to which they can turn to get the portion of the record of knowledge and experience that they cannot get elsewhere. This is the part of the record not aimed at a mass audience, the part that people seek as individuals. Here is the essence of the library, ministering to the searcher alone and unique.[13]

Martin's speech, which was published in *Library Journal*, had a strong and immediate impact on some leaders in the public library community. In 1983, the president of PLA appointed a New Standards Task Force assigned to "develop a preliminary paper outlining possible parameters of new qualitative and quantitative standards for public libraries; to address the identification of research necessary to produce valid standards."[14]

The task force members gave a creative interpretation to that baffling assignment. Instead of fixing their attention on standards, they set out to produce a replacement for *A Planning Process*. This replacement was to guide library planning in accordance with the ideas set forth by Lowell Martin in his Bowker Lecture. The task force called its venture the Public Library Development Program.[15]

About four years elapsed from the time the task force was first appointed until the replacement for *A Planning Process* became available. In the interim, library planners continued to waste their time using *A Planning Process*. If that document was a worthwhile guide to planning, the effort to replace it was itself wasteful. If *A Planning Process* needed replacing, as it did, those directing the replacement project should have said so. The reluctance of library leaders to be forthright in appraising useless documents inflicts a high cost on those who try to use them.

In June 1986, the president-elect of PLA gave a progress report: "The consulting team is developing a role-setting manual which grew in concept out of Lowell Martin's suggestion that libraries should select the roles they can best fulfil for their community."[16] The new manual, scheduled for publication by the middle of the following year, appeared on time. Its title is *Planning and Role Setting for Public Libraries*.

The authors make it clear at the outset that the new manual is "not a revision" of *A Planning Process*. The new document provides "a new approach to public library planning."[17] The authors' indebtedness to Lowell Martin is obvious and fully acknowledged. In the most important chapter, entitled "Developing Roles and Mission," the authors list eight roles. The roles are presented in the authors' own terms but are essentially those identified by Martin. The authors state that no library can play all of the roles; planners must select.

The eight roles are: Community Activities Center, Community Information Center, Formal Education Support Center, Independent Learning Center, Popular Materials Library, Preschoolers' Door to Learning, Reference Library, and Research Center.[18] Four of the eight roles are educational in the old public library tradition. Those four describe educational services for students, for individuals seeking self-education, for children, and for scholars. Of the remaining four roles, one describes traditional reference service, and another special reference service related to "community organizations, issues, and services." Another, Community Activities Center, describes the library as a place for community activities and meetings. And, finally, the role entitled Popular Materials Library describes the library as a provider of "current, high-demand, high-interest materials."[19] The eight roles are described in reasonably clear terms. When the word information is used, its meaning is limited and easy to grasp. None of the roles listed suggest that the library is to provide vitally important service for all the people.

All of the eight roles are essentially traditional. All describe materials and services that public libraries have long provided or sought to provide. The new planning manual thus informs its readers that public library history sets the broad limits within which the institution must work.

Library planners, the document insists, must choose the roles the library is to play. Choices not made deliberately "are made by default." Choices should be determined by "identified community needs."[20]

Prescriptions for assessing community needs are given in another chapter. Planners should take into account demographics, economic and social conditions, and other "information and educational services" available in the community. Unfortunately, the document does not offer any criteria for distinguishing more urgent needs from those that are less urgent. That is one of its flaws.[21]

When library planners have selected roles and established the priority of roles, the planners are ready to formulate the library's mission statement, which identifies "the library's purpose" and "primary and secondary roles." In the example given, the chosen roles are: "Primary: Formal Educational Support Center and Reference Library. Secondary: Preschoolers' Door to Learning and Independent Learning Center." The mission statement given in the example says that the library will "give special emphasis" to helping students at all levels and to "stimulating young children's interests and appreciation for reading and learning."[22] The mission statement incorporates the roles the library has chosen, specifies priorities, and makes it fairly clear what kind of contribution the library will try to make to the community.

The chapter following the one on roles and mission deals with the formulating of goals and objectives. Goals and objectives "should support the roles and mission statement." Objectives should be measurable. Measures stated in the objectives should help planners "assess how well the library is fulfilling its roles."[23]

Planners are advised to formulate objectives with the help of a new edition of the manual mentioned earlier in this chapter, *Output Measures for Public Libraries*. The 1987 edition of *Output Measures* is a companion volume to the new planning document. Both are part of the Public Library Development Project. The new edition of *Output Measures*, designed to be used in conjunction with the new planning document, does not provide any new measures; "the measures remain the same." In the new *Output Measures*, however, the measures are "more closely integrated" with the planning process. It is made clear that measures are useful to the extent that they "reflect the library's mission, roles, goals, and objectives."[24] The principal virtue of the new edition of *Output Measures* is that it definitely assigns to library statistics their proper subordinate role. The new edition is thus a helpful companion to the new planning document we have been discussing.

Following the chapter on goals and objectives, the new planning document concludes with a discussion of the later stages of the planning process. The later chapters, like the earlier, are clear, intelligent, and complete. One cannot find serious fault with the planning scheme the document presents.

Of course the document could have been better. It falls short of its inspiration, the speech given by Lowell Martin. The document presents the eight roles like beads on a string, of more or less equal importance and value, and as matters of local choice. The document fails to point out, as Martin did, that some roles are preferable to others. The document does not identify the "essence" of the public library, serving as an instrument of self-education for "at least some part of the populace." The document does not suggest that the library as a "popular materials" center is superfluous considering today's "communication matrix." The document fails to provide leadership but could easily have done so by simply being more faithful to its source.

At the same time, however, the strengths of the document are such that its effects may exceed the expectations of the authors. Or it may be that the authors are more subtle than they wish to seem. It is true that they offer the role of popular materials library without denigrating that role. However, they insist that community needs must justify selection of that role. Perhaps that is their way of indicating that the popular materials role is superfluous. Let planners try to discover anything resembling a need for such a role. In addition, when pointing out benefits the community might receive from a popular materials library, the authors say, apparently without intending to be sly, that individuals who borrow popular materials are relieved of the need to "purchase these materials" and thus receive an "economic benefit." They also point out that the popular materials role "enhances and supplements" the offerings of "video-outlets and media."[25] The benefits of the role are enough to persuade intelligent planners to rule it out.

Taken as a whole, *Planning and Role Setting for Public Libraries* provides the best official counsel available to the public library community for forty years. It is clear and unpretentious. It urges the primacy of purpose. It does not tempt librarians to courses of action that are self-serving. The document offers the professional community a chance to find a distinctive and valuable place for the library in society, a proper purpose.

A public library as a source of informal self-education for children, students, and adults is a useful and excellent thing. Only a minority uses it. But that minority consists of a great many individuals; and they use the library for something it alone offers.

Librarians have often been told why the taxpayers support the library. The appearance of a good planning document, *Planning and Role Setting for Public Libraries*, provides an occasion for another retelling. Taxpayers support the library because they believe it confers the benefits of knowledge and culture. Taxpayers understand, in an obscure way, that these attainments are of great importance. Apart from their intrinsic excellence, knowledge and culture combat ignorance and barbarism; and taxpayers understand, again in an obscure way, that ignorance and barbarism are hateful and dangerous. Taxpayers may not be deeply interested in knowledge and culture for themselves; but they respect and appreciate the importance of both.

Library history has demonstrated that the library's ability to confer knowledge and culture on the community is limited. Relatively few seek those benefits from an institution that provides no programs, instruction, discipline, recognition, or credentials. The community demonstrates its understanding of the library's limited ability to provide knowledge and culture by the limited level of support it provides. But it also demonstrates its appreciation of the library's importance by the strength and stability of its desire to have one. Trying to turn the library into something other than a provider of knowledge and culture will not increase the community's level of support; that will always be tied to the library's ability to provide those benefits. But turning the library into a fun house or smorgasbord of marginal social services might well diminish the community's desire to have a library. And it is important for the community to have a library, not so that librarians may have jobs, but because knowledge and culture are important to the community. One would expect librarians to appreciate that importance at least as much as the community at large.

It is too soon to tell if the new planning document will set the public library community on the right track. But it is a step in the right direction.

NOTES

1. Anne J. Mathews, "The Use of Marketing Principles in Library Planning," in Darlene E. Weingand, ed. *Marketing for Libraries and Information Agencies* (Norwood, N.J.: Ablex, 1984), 3.

2. Darlene E. Weingand, "The Role of Marketing in the Future of Rural Libraries," *Illinois Libraries* 68 (October 1986): 495, 499.

3. Editorial, *Library Journal* 104 (September 1, 1979): 1605.

4. Judith McPheron, "A Critique of the Progressive Public Library Movement in America," *Illinois Libraries* 59 (April 1977), 300–02.

5. Thomas Ballard, "Four Guidelines for Public Librarianship," *Public Library Quarterly* 3 (Spring-Summer 1982): 17, 21.

6. Murray C. Bob, "The Case for Quality Book Selection," *Library Journal* 107 (September 15, 1982): 1709–10.

7. Lowell A. Martin, "The Public Library: Middle-age Crisis or Old Age," *Library Journal* 108 (January 1, 1983): 20.

8. Ibid., 19.

9. Ibid.

10. Ibid., 20–21.

11. Ibid., 22.

12. Ibid., 21.

13. Ibid., 22.

14. Karen J. Krueger and Douglas L. Zweizig, "Getting It Together: A Report on PLA's Work in Progress," *Illinois Libraries* 66 (May 1984): 233.

15. Ibid., 234.

16. Kathleen Mehaffy Balcom, "To Concentrate and Strengthen," *Library Journal* 111 (June 15, 1986). 38.

17. Charles R. McClure et al., *Planning and Role Setting for Public Libraries* (Chicago: American Library Association, 1987), xix.

18. Ibid., 28.

19. Ibid.

20. Ibid.

21. Ibid., 18.

22. Ibid., 43.

23. Ibid., 45, 53.

24. Nancy Z. Van House et al., *Output Measures for Public Libraries*, 2d ed. (Chicago: American Library Association, 1987), xvii, 2.

25. McClure et al., *Planning and Role Setting for Public Libraries*, 36.

Conclusion

The foregoing history is too long and complicated for a general interpretation in a brief concluding essay. Interpretation, where it seemed important, was provided along the way, in connection with particular developments. Anything more, it seems to this writer, requires a separate project and should not be attempted here. What this concluding note provides, therefore, is no more than a personal view of what the public library community ought to attempt in the remaining years of this century.

The public library community should work to restore the identity of the public library as an institution for informal self-education. This means going back to what made the library grow, develop, and earn the respect and support of the public in the first place. This means setting the library once again to the only task of importance that it ever performed, providing education for those who seek it. This does not mean trying once more to make the library an instrument for the self-education of the masses. That is impossible. The masses have other commitments. Librarians who undertake to restore the identity of the library must do so without the vision that inspired their predecessors, the vision of educating the masses. But those who undertake the restoration also have an advantage. Their efforts to perform their educational task will not be doomed to repeated and inevitable failure.

There is no question of the value of restoring the library to its educational task. Education does not need to prove its value. Education is what the library can provide. Education is what the public wants from the library. The time is ripe for restoration. A step in the right direction has already been taken. The history of the public library argues that restoration is the only course that is worthy, the only course that leads anywhere. The American public has always wanted and still wants the public library to be an educational institution. And, in all probability, the public will not have it otherwise.

Selected Bibliography

Ballard, Thomas H. *The Failure of Resource Sharing in Public Libraries and Alternative Strategies for Service*. Chicago: American Library Association, 1986.

Berelson, Bernard. *The Library's Public*. New York: Columbia University Press, 1949.

Carrier, Esther Jane. *Fiction in Public Libraries: 1876–1900*. New York: Scarecrow Press, 1965.

Chancellor, John, Miriam D. Tompkin, and Hazel I. Medway. *Helping the Reader toward Self-Education*. Chicago: American Library Association, 1938.

A Forum on the Public Library Inquiry: The Conference at the University of Chicago Graduate Library School, August 8–13, 1949, ed. Lester Asheim. New York: Columbia University Press, 1950.

Garrison, Dee. *Apostles of Culture: The Public Librarian and American Society, 1876–1920*. New York: The Free Press, 1979.

Johnson, Alvin. *The Public Library: A People's University*. New York: American Association for Adult Education, 1938.

Leigh, Robert D. *The Public Library in the United States*. New York: Columbia University Press, 1950.

McClure, Charles R. et al. *Planning and Role Setting for Public Libraries*. Chicago: American Library Association, 1987.

U.S. Bureau of Education. *Public Libraries in the United States of America: Their History, Condition and Management, Special Report*. Washington: Government Printing Office, 1876.

Van House, Nancy A., et al. *Output Measures for Public Libraries*. 2d ed. Chicago: American Library Association, 1987.

Whitehill, Walter Muir. *Boston Public Library: A Centennial History*. Cambridge: Harvard University Press, 1956.

Index

About the Author

PATRICK WILLIAMS, Associate Professor of Library Science at Rosary College, is the author of *The Vital Network: A Theory of Communication and Society* (Greenwood Press, 1978) and other publications.

www.ingramcontent.com/pod-product-compliance
Lightning Source LLC
Chambersburg PA
CBHW070442100426
42812CB00004B/1185